THE ART HANDBOOK for PHOTOGRAPHING Their Own ARTWORK

THE ARTISTS'
HANDBOOK
for
PHOTOGRAPHING
Their Own
ARTWORK

JOHN WHITE

Crown Trade Paperbacks, New York

Published by Crown Publishers, Inc., 201 East 50th Street, New York, New York 10022.

Member of the Crown Publishing Group.

Random House, Inc. New York, Toronto, London, Sydney, Auckland

CROWN TRADE PAPERBACKS and colophon are trademarks of Crown Publishers, Inc.

Manufactured in the United States of America

Design by Lenny Henderson

Library of Congress Cataloging-in-Publication Data

White, John,

The artists' handbook for photographing their own artwork / by John White.—1st ed.

Includes index.

1. Photography of art.   I. Title.

TR657.W49 1994

778.9'97—dc20   93-21221

CIP

ISBN 0-517-88174-8

10 9 8 7 6 5 4 3 2 1

First Edition

Contents

Introduction

Photography can be one of the most powerful and useful tools for advancing your art career and reaching a wide audience. Artists need photographs for many reasons: to apply for grants, to send to galleries, for announcements, for portfolios of finished work; and for documentation of work in progress.

Unfortunately, bad photogaphs can detract from even the most splendid art. Gallery owners admit that they sometimes judge the quality of the photography as much as that of your art, since photographs are often the only way they can review your work.

This book will be an essential guide for artists who want to shoot their own high-quality transparencies, which are the most requested as well as the best type of film for art documentation. The goal of the book is to advise you how to keep equipment and material costs down while learning how to take the best photographs possible.

I personally use every method described here, having found them simple and effective. You will learn that using a proven lighting method is half the battle. Just look for the chapter that covers your type of art and you will find diagrams, photos, and hints that make the lighting setup perfectly clear and straightforward.

Learning the strategies that produce consistent image quality is the other, more elusive half of the battle. Much of this book focuses on to how to keep all the photographic variables working for you. Chapter 10, a detailed troubleshooting section, written in nontechnical language, will help you identify the likely causes of less than perfect results.

There are no shortcuts to producing professional-quality photographs. No magic, either. Even with the help of this book, you still have to do the necessary work and follow-up to get the results you desire. But you will tremendously shorten the time it takes to get from neophyte to wizard—even a quick scan of this book will show that doing high-quality work is well within your means and ability. After one evening reading the book, you'll probably be ready to set up your first test shot. Because the guides and checklists keep you on course and away from the usual hazards, you won't have to reinvent the wheel at every stage. A few more evenings of serious work should bring your photography within striking distance of the highest standard.

Even though this book starts at the most basic level, it is detailed and thorough enough to serve as a reference book for artists with more advanced photographic skills who wish to begin shooting artwork professionally.

1

Camera and Lighting Equipment

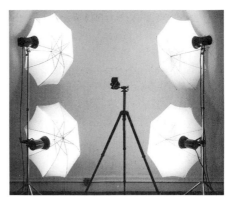

What You Need and How It Works

The best advice I can give people about cameras and other photo equipment is not to be intimidated by them. You can achieve splendid results with the most basic and primitive equipment if you know what you are doing, and this book will show you how.

How Cameras Work
Why Things Click

Let's begin with a review of how cameras function. For our purposes, the typical camera must have three simple components: a *lens* that admits light through a *shutter* or some other means of controlling the amount of light falling onto the *film*, which records the image.

Once film is in the camera, it is typically less complicated to operate than many appliances, notably VCRs or microwaves, although you may not think so after reading the camera's operating manual. If you are graduating from amateur, "point and shoot" cameras, make sure you read and comprehend this section before opening your camera's manual.

Although cameras are mechanically and sometimes electronically complex pieces of equipment, don't let this intimidate you. There are only two controls that are essential for operating a camera properly and obtaining professional results: *shutter speed* and *aperture*. Together, these two variables determine the film's *exposure* to light and needs to be critically controlled. Make sure that your camera allows you at least some method of selecting each of these controls individually.

Shutter Speeds
An Open and Shut Case

The camera's shutter is similar to one on a window except that it must block out all light and is closed most of the time to protect the film from unwanted exposure. Setting the *shutter speed* controls the amount of time the shutter will remain open upon release. The longer the shutter remains open, the greater the quantity of light that strikes the film; more light produces "lighter" results in the final image. The shorter the duration, the smaller the quantity of light that strikes the film, producing a "darker" result.

Exposure is cumulative in this sense. Some cameras will allow you to repeatedly expose the same piece of film. Each re-exposure will add to the final total of light, but only up to a point. It is like adding gas to your car: the tank has a finite capacity. You can put in various amounts, but there is a limit to how much it can hold. Each film, by design, has a limit to the total amount of light it can be exposed to before it becomes unusable. A typical shutter speed indicator on a camera may read:

B 1 2 4 8 15 30 60 125 500 1000 2000

The numbers are really fractions. The 2000 indicates 1/2000 of a second shutter speed. The 1000 is actually 1/1000 of a second and allows the light double the time to pass through to the film than does the 2000 setting. The rest of the speeds follow suit: going to the next slower speed doubles the total film exposure, while choosing the next fastest speed cuts the film exposure in half. "B" stands for *bulb*. This term is a throwback to the earliest days of photography when the first shutters were controlled by air pressure. When squeezed, a rubber bulb, via a hose, provided the pressure to open the shutter until pressure was released, closing the shutter. In today's cameras, this setting keeps the shutter open as long as the shutter release button is held down, enabling the user to create longer shutter exposures than those indicated on the dial.

Aperture Settings
An Eye-Opening Exposé

Our other means of setting the exposure is called the *aperture*, an adjustable hole between the elements of the lens that regulates the amount of light passing through to the film. The aperture settings are called f-stops and are indicated on a band around the lens. A typical lens has markings:

1.4   2   2.8   4   5.6   8   11   16   22

←—— Larger apertures   Smaller apertures ——→

As with the shutter speeds we have discussed, changing the aperture from one f-stop to an adjacent f-stop doubles or halves the exposure, depending on the direction. Most manufacturers have intermediate settings (or are continuously variable) between the marked f-stops for finer adjustment of exposure.

You may think that the changes in both shutter speed and aperture seem rather coarse, 50 to 100 percent, considering what precise and expensive instruments cameras are. But the changes are more subtle than the numbers suggest: when asked to indicate a halving or doubling in the intensity of a light, most people are off by a factor of thirty!

Since aperture and shutter speeds vary by the same percentage, there is an established relationship between the two and it is shown as:

shutter speeds

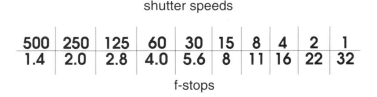

500	250	125	60	30	15	8	4	2	1
1.4	2.0	2.8	4.0	5.6	8	11	16	22	32

f-stops

In each of these combinations, *the total exposure to the film is exactly the same!* The combination using 1/500th of a second for the shutter and f1.4 will produce an image exposure exactly equal to one shot with the combination 1/4th of a second using f16. In photographic terms, we call each of these exposures *equivalent*.

Light Meters
Getting Right with Light

A *light meter* is used to determine accurately the correct exposure settings. A typical meter, facing page, shows the same correlation between shutter speed and aperture.

Many cameras have the meters built into the camera itself with interconnections to the shutter speed and aperture. These light meters measure the *reflected* light from the subject to the lens. These meters have become very accurate and dependable, but they need to be used with knowledge of their capabilities and limitations.

Handheld light meters may measure reflected light, or *incident* light (the light falling onto the subject), or both, making them more versatile. Using a handheld meter in combination with a built-in meter provides a backup, allowing greater flexibility in choosing the optimum measurement method.

With few exceptions, all meters are geared to measure the middle range of reflectance—generally 18 percent—producing what we call medium or *photographic gray*. Whenever light strikes any object, it can be either reflected or absorbed. In the typical outdoor scenic, only 18 percent of the light is reflected back to the camera while the other 82 percent is being absorbed by objects in the scene. Like middle C on a piano, photographic gray is the middle of a range of tones from pure white to the densest black.

Take a good look at the middle gray in figure 1.2. That is what your meter "thinks" the world looks like. If used randomly in a variety of situations, the meter will be accurate about 60 per-

Figure 1.1. Three examples of light meters. Left to right: reflected, incident, and electronic flash.

cent of the time, which is not quite up to professional standards. Later chapters will cover how to use your meter with precision in every lighting set-up described.

Image Quality
Looking and Feeling Sharp

The *quality* of the image is determined more by aperture choice than shutter speed for two reasons:

1. manufacturers design their lenses to optimize a certain aperture or range of apertures;
2. aperture choice determines where the zone of sharpness within a picture begins and ends at the point of focus.

Always adjust the aperture to control the image and adjust the shutter speed to control movement or vibration. In all the situations in this book, we will want to control the way the image "looks" by first selecting the best aperture.

A lens set at f1.4 has a very narrow field of focus

x...x

compared to a lens set at f16

x.........................x

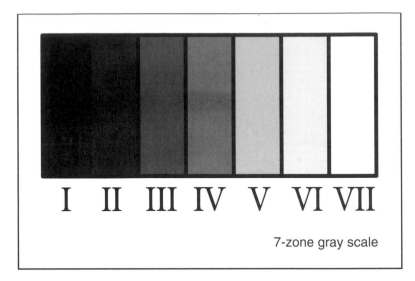

I   II   III   IV   V   VI   VII

7-zone gray scale

Figure 1.2. Seven-zone photographic gray scale.

In each case, the end point is the closest and the furthest position relative to the camera where an object at the edges of that field begins to loose sharpness or look blurry. Anything within the zone will be reasonably if not perfectly sharp up to the limits of the lens's capabilities. This zone of sharpness from the point nearest the camera (foreground) to the point farthest from the camera (background) is called *depth of field* (figure 1.3). Many lenses have permanent scale markings adjacent to the f-stop ring to indicate depth of field. *For any given aperture, the depth of field extends one-third toward the camera and two-thirds behind the point of focus.*

Behind the point of focus, everything in the image becomes progressively smaller. The mere act of reduction will make anything look sharper. In front of the point of focus, everything in the image becomes progressively larger, essentially magnifying the lack of sharpness; this explains the need for a two-to-one differential between, behind, and in front of the point of focus. The focus setting that is one-third the distance maximizes the sharpness potential.

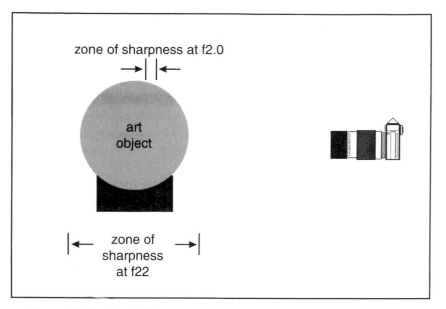

Figure 1.3. Depth of field.

Some cameras allow you to look directly through the lens at different apertures and actually preview the depth of field. Producing an effect similar to squinting with the naked eye, the image appears progressively darker the smaller the aperture, but objects will appear sharper.

Choosing the Right Lens
The Long and the Short of It

Another factor in depth of field is the *focal length* of the lens. This is the distance from the optical center of the lens to the film plane and is usually measured in millimeters, or mm. Many camera bodies can accommodate a number of lenses that vary in focal length.

A normal lens for any camera is approximately equal to the diagonal of its film image size. For a 35mm camera, the image size is 24mm × 36mm. The diagonal of the film is 43mm: a normal lens for 35mm cameras is therefore 43mm. Early manufacturers found it much easier and less costly to produce "faster" (larger aperture) lenses a few millimeters longer. The 50mm standard for normal lenses carries over to modern times.

When looking through the camera with a normal lens attached, you will be able to see any object in front of the camera that is within approximately 20 degrees from the center of the lens axis, creating a 46-degree view *diagonally* across the frame. The picture area any lens can "see" and record on film is called *angle of view* (figure 1.4). For normal lenses, this is about 20 degrees on either side of the center, and about 14 degrees off center, top to bottom. These figures are usually consolidated and expressed as 46 degrees for a normal lens on the diagonal, which is the standard measurement used by manufacturers. (See figure1.4.)

Wide-angle lenses have shorter focal lengths than the normal-angle lenses for 35mm are:

35mm	**62-degree angle**
28mm	**72-degree angle**
20mm	**90-degree angle**

Since these lenses "see" a broader area, they are useful in cramped spaces or for exaggerating near-far relationships. The shorter the focal length, the greater the exaggeration. Depth of field increases, too. Wide angle is often used in architectural interiors when a physical restriction, like a wall, prevents backing up far enough to include everything you want to have in the frame area. In such a situation, you would change to a short enough focal length lens to take in the area you need to cover.

An advertising or editorial photographer in the same situation will use a shorter focal length lens for effect, since it can also be used to make small spaces appear larger. The photo of a cabin on a cruise ship can easily be made to look like a stateroom for the brochure.

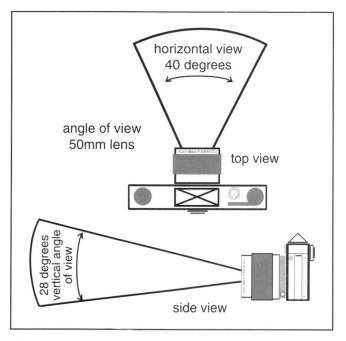

Figure 1.4. Angle of view.

Telephoto lenses have longer focal lengths than a normal lens and are usually optically compacted to produce a smaller, lighter lens. Examples of telephoto lenses for 35mm cameras are:

85mm	**23-degree angle of view**
105mm	**18-degree angle of view**
135mm	**13-degree angle of view**
200mm	**8-degree angle of view**

As focal length increases, the angle of view decreases and the perspective flattens. Depth of field decreases, too. Telephoto lenses are typically used to make distant objects appear closer. Fashion photographers use 180mm to 300mm lenses for the

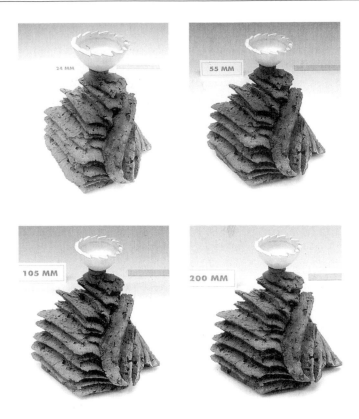

Figure 1.5A–D. Four portraits of a ceramic object taken with 24mm, 55mm, 105mm, and 200mm lenses, respectively, to show the different perspectives produced by various focal lengths. The image distortion is quite noticeable with the 24mm and 200mm lens. Note the differing amounts of background each lens produces.

flattened perspective and for ease in throwing the background out of focus. Unfortunately, these lenses make human beings appear heavier and thicker as focal length increases.

At the shorter end of this category is the *portrait lens*. This is the optimum lens to use for a head-and-shoulder shot and is roughly double the diagonal of the format. For a 35mm camera this would work out to be 43mm × 2 = 86mm. The shorter telephotos (85–105mm) produce natural perspective at a moderate range of 4 to 6 feet. To illustrate the differences, the series of photos (see figure 1.5) keeps the object size constant but changes focal length.

The portrait lens allows a photographer to fill the frame completely with a tight headshot without creating an exaggerated perspective (bigger nose and forehead) because the subject is 3 to 5 feet away from the camera.

This distance creates a "comfort" zone between the photographer and the subject. It also allows the lighting to be positioned closer to the subject and lens axis, making it ideal for photographing three-dimensional art objects.

The Single Lens Reflex
The Best Camera for All Reasons

The most practical camera to start photographing your artwork with is a 35mm SLR, or *single lens reflex* camera. There is only one lens mounted on the camera and it is used alternately for viewing the image or exposing the film. This is accomplished by a mirror behind the lens that diverts the actual image to the viewfinder for you to see and study; when you push the shutter release, the mirror swings up and out of the way to allow the image to pass directly to the film plane. After the shutter opens and closes, the mirror flops down and the photographer is once again looking through the lens. This all takes place in about one-tenth of a second.

The 35mm SLR's versatility lies in it's interchangeable lenses and the availability of a wide variety of films, especially transparency films that when mounted in 2 × 2-inch slide frames, can be easily handled, stored, viewed, or projected. For the artist, these slides are the cheapest way of making color originals and involve the least amount of hassle.

35mm SLR cameras come in a large variety of types. The high-end, feature-laden automatic cameras can operate one or more of the variables for you, setting the aperture or shutter, or both. Many of these cameras will even focus the lens and set the film speed by reading the bar code on the film cassette, including the focus. These technological marvels usually take the operator out of the command loop and are referred to by manufacturers as "Ph.D." cameras," as in "push here, dummy." The inexperienced user will take a quantum leap forward in image quality with no investment in photo theory.

But automatic cameras won't take better pictures than a completely manual camera, where all the exposure options are set by the operator. The automatic type just insures a better chance of obtaining a usable image if you don't know what you are doing. For our purposes, the automatic types may impose an additional burden and inconvenience because the systems can be difficult or impossible to override (how to do this will be discussed in chapters 3 and 4).

Automatic cameras are no substitute for skill and vision. It is necessary to understand all of the camera's functions, automatic or manual, so that you can predict and control the photographic results. If at all possible, you should try to start out using a manually operated, rather than an automatic, camera.

Unfortunately, because of trends toward automation in the amateur market, there are fewer new manual cameras manufactured today, and the majority of these are aimed at the professional market, at "professional" prices. The good news is that there is plenty of secondhand equipment to be found at quite reasonable prices, much of it hardly used at all by people trading their equipment in for Ph.D.-type cameras. The robust construction and overall versatility of these professional manual cameras make them a long-term bargain, even if purchased new. My twenty-year-old, heavily used manual cameras will still be earning their living into the next century.

Tremendous Photo Secret Revealed

The overall quality of the optical and mechanical characteristics of cameras and lenses have improved over the last ten years, creating an almost level playing field among the major manufacturers. Great results can be had with just about any modern camera. Most people overlook the obvious (and for some purposes, essential) piece of equipment that will help ensure the optimal results promised by all that design and engineering: a good tripod.

It may not be the "sexiest" piece of equipment on which to spend money, but you will understand the importance of using a good tripod after you carefully examine the photographic results. A sturdy tripod can help deliver the optical quality you pay so much for in good lenses by minimizing camera movement and dampening vibration. The benefit of working with a camera on a tripod is that you can analyze the framing, composition, and lighting of a setup carefully before taking the picture. Then it is simple to produce several *identical* pictures, a common and necessary practice for recording artwork.

Summing Up

The following is the minimum camera equipment needed on hand to do the work described in this book. Depending on the type of artwork to be photographed, other specialized equipment may be required. Be sure to read the chapter dealing with your particular type of artwork before getting started. In general you will need:

1. 35mm single lens reflex with a normal 50mm lens
2. Moderate telephoto lens, 85 to 105mm
3. Handheld or built-in light meter
4. Sturdy tripod

This equipment list represents a *considerable and serious* purchase. But if you can't afford the top equipment, don't let lack of money stop you, because it is important to have your work seen.

There are a lot of secondhand, hardly used cameras on the market, most of them at a fraction of their original selling price. Or someone you know may have equipment that you can borrow. Start with your immediate family and work outward.

Work with other artists who have the same photographic needs. What one may not have, the other may be able to get. Several artists can build a whole network and bring down costs by sharing them.

If you are in school, you may be able to borrow equipment from the photo department and use their other resources while you are at it. Many communities have photo cooperatives that you can join at a modest cost and rent both equipment and facilities to get the job done (often with friendly technical assistance on hand).

In most larger cities, rental equipment is readily available. Many stores rent the latest equipment on a daily or weekly basis. They will give you back a percentage (if not all) of the rental fee toward the purchase of that or similar equipment within a certain time period, usually thirty days. Most photo stores won't take back purchased equipment that you don't like once you've used it, so renting is a great way of seeing if an item really meets your needs and does everything it is supposed to do. There are even a few companies that will allow you to rent via UPS—get a few fellow artists together, split the cost, and you can shoot your artwork very inexpensively. When you've sold six pieces of your art from your photos, go out and buy everything you want.

Lighting
Achieving Divine Illumination

This book is designed to help you achieve consistent, professional photographic reproductions of your artwork. The easiest and best way to make that possible is to create the appropriate lighting for the photograph. The additional equipment needed depends on the type of art being photographed and will be covered in chapters on different types of art. The price range for this equipment varies a great deal. You don't necessarily need to use expensive equipment to get professional results, but you do need to be consistent.

Generally speaking, natural light is not desirable for photographing artwork because it varies so much in intensity, quality, and color. Natural light can be harsh (no clouds at noon) or soft (overcast), warm or cool. Meanwhile, photographic color film is locked into a specific color temperature and sensitivity that can't be changed. Providing à constant light source to use with a constant film source, results can be predicted and controlled. It may take a test or two to get everything perfect, but after that it's just a matter of following the protocol.

The earliest photographers quickly discovered the need to augment natural light to get predictable results. Burning magnesium powder in an open wooden trough, they were able to generate an explosive "flash" of light that lasted about one second and could be quite dangerous. There were no viable alternatives, candles and lamplight output being very weak and electric light bulbs just an idea in Mr. Edison's mind.

The real problem was that film was not very sensitive in those days, often requiring up to one-minute-long exposures. Shutters were not invented or needed—exposure began when the lens cap was taken off and ended when it was put back on. Burning the magnesium flash powder did allow for a form of "instantaneous" photography, since most people could stand still and keep their eyes open for a second. Although primitive by today's standards, this equipment could, nonetheless, produce stunning results in the hands of talented practitioners.

A refined form of this lighting, the flashbulb, remained popular as recently as twenty-five years ago. The magnesium was encased in a glass bulb to contain the discharge. The flashbulb was small, powerful, lightweight, and its fixture could easily be built into the most basic of cameras. The downside was the high cost per unit, the heat it generated, and the still present danger of explosions.

Modern Lighting
A Current Affair

There are two basic types of modern photographic lighting equipment: tungsten or electronic flash, and both are pretty old technologies. *Tungsten* lighting has been around for nearly a century as the common household light bulb. Light bulbs work by passing an electric current through a thin wire or filament. The filament heats up to a very high temperature and emits light. For our purposes, we want to use special photographic bulbs that have a specific color output that matches our film. In use, these electric bulbs constantly emit light, so what we see is what we get.

Electronic flash, developed in the 1930s by Dr. Harold Edgerton at MIT, differs from tungsten because it emits a pulse of light that varies in duration (anywhere from 1/90th of a second to 1/50,000th of a second) and must be synchronized to the shutter. An electric charge is built up in a storage device (a capacitor), then dumped instantaneously to the flashtube, whose element heats up very quickly to produce light. The duration is far too short (typically less than 1/180th of a second) and the light is much too bright to see more than a searing flash, when what is really needed is to comprehend and critically assess the light's direction and placement.

To solve this problem for studio photographers, flash manufacturers have added a low-output tungsten light (called a modeling lamp) to the flash head so that the photographer has a general idea what the lighting looks like. The complexity of this arrangement and the other functions of modern-day equipment add considerably to both cost and bulk. Special light meters (again, on the pricey side) are needed to measure the flash output and a Polaroid test shot (requiring a special camera or adaptor back) must be done for on-the-spot assessment of the actual lighting.

All this gives you greater flexibility, greater power output, lower operating costs, and lower operating temperatures. Because this equipment is complex, its purchase price is generally higher by a factor of at least two. The additional initial expense can be easily justified if the equipment will be heavily used.

All the lighting techniques described in this book are readily interchangeable between tungsten and flash. If this is your first effort at photographic lighting, you will probably be better off beginning with tungsten lighting since the investment is really quite modest. Once you understand the basics, it will be much easier to learn and comprehend electronic flash techniques. For class demonstration purposes I always use tungsten, since the constant light is easier to see and understand. Seeing is believing.

Color Temperature
Not All Light Is Equal

Photographic tungsten lamps are designed to emit light at a certain color temperature, which is expressed in a scientific standard of degrees Kelvin (abbreviated °K and derived by heating platinum to a certain temperature and measuring the light emitted in reference to the visible spectrum). We see light through our eyes from about 2000°K (the red end of the spectrum) to 7000°K (the blue/violet end of the spectrum). Photo lamps are usually designed to produce light at 3200°K or 3400°K. To reproduce color faithfully, you must use a film balanced for the same color temperature (clearly marked on both the film box and cassette as being 3200°K type B, or 3400°K type A).

Daylight, however, registers at about 5500°K, and since it is the most abundant supply of light on this planet it gets the most abundant supply of film. The box and the cartridge simply say "daylight." Unless you use a specific color conversion filter, daylight film shot under tungsten light produces a heavy orange or salmon cast. Tungsten film shot with a daylight light source will have a heavy bluish cast. Neither example will do much for your artwork.

Your brain is able to judge the color scale correctly under a wide variety of light sources. It is so adept, in fact, that we are hardly conscious of any transition from one light source to another. But turn on a household lamp (about 2600°K) next to a window during the day and compare their relative color with the sky. Quite a difference!

Color film is mechanically locked into responding correctly to only one color temperature light source. No mixing allowed. (We can easily avoid mixing light sources by working in a darkened room or waiting until it is dark outside or both). Since we are using tungsten lamps, we must match it exactly to a tungsten-balanced film of the same color temperature. Another option is to use a daylight film and put the appropriate conversion filter on the lens at the cost of about two-thirds of a stop in speed.

Tungsten Lighting Equipment

Inexpensive
$10–$30 each, with bulb

The least expensive lighting equipment is nothing more than a socket/reflector into which we screw a photo bulb. The least expensive of this type have a spring clamp arrangement so that you can attach it to any makeshift support. You can generally interchange the reflectors from 5 inches to about 12 inches. The bulbs will be limited in power to 250 watts or 500 watts and will have a useful life of 8 to 12 hours.

Although the cheapest, this type of lighting equipment is excellent for most smaller flat artwork, up to 16 × 20 inches, jewelry, and smaller three-dimensional pieces. Using several in combination will enable you to photograph much larger pieces, too. Equipment in this price range will not take much abuse, but, as it is so inexpensive, accidentally breaking it is no big deal. Accessories are generally nonexistent since they would be much more costly to make than light itself. Neither of these shortcomings may matter to you, depending on the type of work involved.

Moderate
$45–$65 each, with bulb; accessories extra

The next step up is a more robust version of the above. They are constructed using heavier-gauge materials and can withstand considerable usage. In addition, you will be able to purchase accessories, like diffusion screens, grids, and barn doors, that help control the light and may be necessary to photograph your particular artwork. This type of equipment is designed to mount securely on a light stand.

Quartz
$65–$200 each, with lamp; accessories extra

One more notch up in expense and flexibility gets quartz-powered lamps that are very small, yet have a very high output (up to 2000 watts). These lamps are quite a bit more expensive, but have a much longer useful life (200 hours). The reflectors designed for these lamps are much more efficient than those previously mentioned, enabling you to use either a smaller aperture and/or a faster shutter speed.

These units generally have enough accessories available to match any need, including filter holders to convert the light to a daylight color temperature (at the expense of a little over two stops in light output—so you really need the extra power). This quality of equipment is used not only by professional art photographers, but also TV crews and photographers who specialize in architectural interiors. Both need to augment the existing light without overpowering it. It is not uncommon for any of them to have six to ten of these lighting units as well as several specialized lights, accessories, and stands.

Care and Handling
The Hands-off Approach

The one thing in common to all of these tungsten lamps is that *they all generate enough heat to easily burn you.* Photographers call this type of lighting "hot light," and for good reason. Buying and wearing a good pair of cotton or leather work gloves to handle or adjust these lights will literally save your skin.

When working with the higher-powered lamps, it's a good idea to know where the fuse or circuit breaker box is located before you switch on the lights, especially in multilight setups. Many draw more than the 15-amp limit common in residential units, making it easy to overload any one circuit. Use heavy-duty extension cords to get the lights on as many different circuits as possible (if you blow the circuits out in this scenario, you better have a flashlight handy, too).

Quartz lamps are expensive to replace. Their operating life can be shortened by fingerprints on the bulb itself. Install these lamps wearing cotton gloves and inspect for cleanliness on a regular basis.

All bulbs are most fragile when they are cooling down; rough handling at this point could break the filament. It's a good practice to let your equipment cool completely before packing and transporting.

As with cameras, it's not the light that's important, it's how you use it. Used properly, no one can tell, by the photograph, if your equipment costs $25 or $25,000.

2
Film
and
Processing

Accentuating the Positive

As I mentioned earlier, most artists are typically required to submit color transparencies for grants, shows, galleries, and reproduction. This is fortunate for three reasons: (1) transparencies inherently contain more photographic information, such as brightness ranges and detail, than prints, which are second generation; (2) it's the cheapest way to shoot color; and (3) there is no temptation to process the film yourself. Reason 3 alone will save you a great deal of time and almost all of the grief. Trained technicians with hundreds of thousands of dollars' worth of equipment have a hard enough time keeping the color right, so it's best to leave that challenge to the experts. We'll talk about finding the color lab of your dreams later.

Transparency film isn't the only film in town. You may need to shoot with another type of film to fulfill a specific assignment. By comparison, all films other than transparency are more forgiving and easier to use.

Transparency film is an exacting film to shoot because the end product is the original piece of film that goes through your camera. The color, exposure, composition, and contrast have to be perfect when the shutter is clicked. You don't have to be a rocket scientist to get it right, because a lot of guys in the white lab coats work day and night to make your photographic life as simple as possible. You just have to understand the system.

Film Theory
Guesswork Not Allowed

After twenty-three years of studying, the photographic process can still feel magical to me. But there is no trick to how the system works.

All general-purpose color films can be divided into two categories. *Negative films* produce images exactly opposite to our perceptions of reality. (The lightest areas appear the darkest, the darkest areas have the least density, and the colors don't make sense to even experienced photographers like me.) The image is reversed again when the negative is used to make a photographic print, whose colors and tones approximate the original subject matter. The printing of the negative offers not only an opportunity to correct color, contrast, and density but also to enhance or alter the image.

The second category, *reversal films*, also known as *transparency films*, produce direct positive images that we view by passing light through the film. This type of film reacts to light just like negative films and indeed produce at first a negative image that is then chemically or physically (by re-exposure to light) reversed to produce a film positive.

Both transparency and negative color films are made with several layers in their emulsion. There is one layer sensitive to blue, one layer sensitive to green, and one layer sensitive to red. Red, green, and blue are called the *additive primaries*. When equally combined as light they produce an approximation of white light, and mixing them in various combinations allows for the creation of light of any other color.

In transparency film the blue-sensitive layer produces the opposite color dye of yellow (green/red); the green-sensitive layer produces magenta (red/blue) dyes; and the red-sensitive layer produces a cyan (green/blue) dye. Cyan, magenta, and yellow are called *subtractive primaries*. All of these dyes in the film transmit at least two-thirds of the spectrum, allowing some light to pass through each layer of the film. The combination of these three dye layers create the spectrum of color that we see in the processed transparency.

If additive primary dyes (red, green, blue) were used

instead, each film layer would transmit only one specific part of the light spectrum and absorb the rest. Any combination of two additive primary dye layers creates a very effective light barrier and would appear as solid black. For this reason, no color transparency film can be made using the additive primary dyes.

Anyone working with watercolors will be familiar with the subtractive primaries arrangement (although many manufacturers still fudge the labels on small sets, calling their magenta red and their cyan blue). For any specific color, this combination of dyes may not produce an exact replication of the actual wavelength as scientifically metered; it may just give the appearance of that specific color to your amazingly adaptable eye.

Sometimes we can't maintain the illusion of correct color, given the technology of our available film. It's mostly in the very subtle mixture of colors that this system can go awry, and even then it's usually only the artist who will notice the difference. Even when these subtle colors photograph well, there may be problems if the film is ever reproduced by standard four-color printing (that uses cyan, magenta, yellow, and black ink dot combinations to fool the eye into seeing the color spectrum).

Try to remember that there are inherent limitations in a printing process that is just putting different colored dots on white paper. In addition, the final product is at least two generations away from the original transparency. New computer imaging technologies make it possible to manipulate or enhance the printing separations, but this is a pretty expensive option. In this day and age of tight budgets, it is best to get your work published any way you can and have as many people come see the real thing—or the next best thing, an original transparency.

Why There Is No "Perfect" Film

Film manufacturers spend a lot of time and money developing and producing each new film. Their final color balance is often chosen subjectively to produce pleasing or enhanced flesh tones, because a vast majority of all the photos include at least one person.

That's good news if the majority of your work has flesh colors. However, there are many different ideas on the market about what is a pleasing color balance. A lot of these variations are cultural, based on the country where the film is made. In addition, there are the limitations of the commercial dyes available and the chemical processes used.

Just realize that there are no perfect films on the market. There are really a lot of great films, and many will do a perfectly adequate job in nearly all situations. Just expect the unexpected from time to time. Try some other film if you are not getting the results you want after exhausting other means of controlling color balance (see chapter 10, page 225).

Determining Film Speed

There are generally two film standards that indicate the relative sensitivity of film to light. ISO (for International Organization for Standardization) is a numerical system and the American standard. The constants in this standard are:

1. f16
2. an "average" outdoor scene
3. clear, sunny day at noon

The variable in the equation is the shutter speed that would produce the right density for any given film that was properly developed. For example, if a shutter speed of 1/125th of a second worked best with the above constants, the film would be rated at ISO 125; if 1/400th worked the best, the film would be rated at ISO 400, and so on. This makes it very easy for you to give your meter a quick test anytime you are outdoors.

The other standard is DIN (for *Deutsche Industrie-Normen*) and is the common standard in Europe and the rest of the world. DIN numbers have two digits and are designated by a degree symbol. The scale on most meters starts at 10, equivalent to ISO 8. Each increasing number after 10 represents one-third f-stop increase in film sensitivity. For example,

DIN 19° is equivalent to ISO 64; DIN 20° is ISO 80; DIN 21° is ISO 100; and DIN 22° is ISO 125.

Fortunately, most films have marking for both numbers. Make sure that you set the light meter accordingly. On all the new cameras for the American market, the built-in meter uses ISO. Older meters and cameras may have markings for **ASA** (American Standards Association). Regarding film speeds, ISO and ASA are interchangeable. Every modern handheld meter I have found has a scale for both ISO and DIN.

How Film Speed Affects Image Qualities

The following list of film characteristic are generalities. There will be many exceptions, especially between films of different manufacturers.

SLOWER FILMS	FASTER FILMS
ISO /ASA 25–64	**ISO /ASA 160–400**
1. Smaller grain	1. Larger grain
2. Greater sharpness	2. Lower sharpness
3. Better color saturation	3. Lower saturation
4. Smoother gradations	4. Lower contrast

We can conclude from this comparison that the slower films generally produce better images than faster films. In practice, you should use the slowest film that you possibly can.

Each color film is designed to be operated within a certain range of shutter speeds. This information is always listed with the data sheet that is boxed with your film. If you operate outside the film's parameters and use exposures that are too long or too short, you may not get the expected result. This effect is known as *reciprocity failure*. It may be necessary to increase exposure and/or add filtration. Professional tungsten films will list these corrections for you somewhere on its data sheet. Beyond a certain point, proper color balance may not be possible or predictable.

For most of the films you will be using, that point is about one-tenth of a second or slower. Therefore, use a film that will give you at least one-eighth of a second (most cameras don't have one-tenth) at the optimum aperture. This also means that the greater the output of your lighting equipment, the slower the film you can use.

For flat artwork, the optimum aperture is two to four stops down from the maximum. With an f2.8 lens, the best aperture will generally be in the f5.6–f11 range. For three-dimensional work, smaller apertures may be needed to get the required depth of field—plan for f11–f22. If you can't achieve these minimums with a slower speed film, find a faster film that will. If the photographic results are not to your liking, try using bulbs or lamps of higher output that will allow you to use a slower film.

Facts You Won't Find on the Data Sheet
Fine Print Excluded

Optimum Shutter Speeds

Another generalization that is appropriate is: use a slower shutter speed instead of a faster speed whenever possible with color films. Some very well known color photographers are loathe to use shutter speeds faster than 1/30th of a second. It's been claimed, and my experience confirms, that one gets better color saturation and balance with slow shutter speeds. On a tripod, I use 1/30th of a second when possible. With a handheld camera, I use the lowest speed that will guarantee me adequate sharpness. This is a function of the focal length. A rule of thumb is to use at least the fraction of the focal length; a 50mm lens needs 1/50th of a second or faster: a 135mm lens needs 1/135th of a second or faster.

Using faster speeds (1/500th and faster) usually shifts the overall color balance toward blue. You have probably experienced this if you have ever used an electronic flash unit, either built-in or designed to be mounted directly onto the camera, which automatically sets the exposure for you by varying the duration of the flash. Even though the shutter is synchronized and set at 1/60th of a second, the actual exposure speed can be as little as 1/50,000 of a second, making for a heavy bluish cast in slides. Using any flash at its maximum output (and therefore at its longest duration) helps to minimize this problem.

Professional Films

A film labeled "professional" does not guarantee better images, but it almost certainly guarantees higher prices. What you are supposed to get for the extra money is more quality control (25 percent of the cost of any film) along with better and more stringent handling of the product. To get a professional film franchise, dealers must meet certain requirements, the most important of which is having the facilities to refrigerate all the color film stock. This keeps the film from degrading due to heat and humidity. Do not buy any professional color film, regardless of the expiration date, from a dealer who does not refrigerate the film. You will be wasting your money.

Amateur color films are made to be slightly more tolerant of abusive handling, but even they can be destroyed by excessive heat. Because manufacturers allow a more permissive latitude in "acceptable" results with amateur films, expect to see a bit more variation from batch to batch and a longer expiration date.

Storage

Professional film data sheets packed with color film recommend "keep cool/process promptly." It's wise to refrigerate your film until use, allowing one hour to warm it up to room temperature before opening the box. This will prevent any condensation (visible moisture) from appearing on the cartridge or the film itself because of the temperature difference. Some films react badly to humidity—condensation is nothing more than a very localized, very humid situation.

If you don't have an hour to bring the film to room temperature, open the box but do not break the seal of the foil and/or canister. Put this in your pants, skirt, or jacket pocket for ten to fifteen minutes and that will usually do the trick; 4×5 sheet film should be left in the box, of course, and is more comfortably fitted under the arm.

If you cannot process your 35mm color film by the next day, put it back into the canister, making sure that the lid is closed securely. You can now keep the film refrigerated, bringing it to room temperature an hour before processing.

Black-and-white film benefits from the same care and handling. It, too, is sensitive to heat and humidity, but has a much wider latitude since there are no color shifts to worry about. Refrigeration just extends its already long shelf life.

You can also freeze most films. I like to think of this as suspended animation. Film kept years past the expiration date will produce perfect results as long as you have kept it frozen. Allow just a bit more thaw time.

Processing

Choosing the Right Lab

In a perfect world, everyone would have a great photo lab around the corner that provides turnaround times of two hours, at low prices, with color balance and film speed always on the mark. In Manhattan, my lab came close (except for the high prices), having only two notable slip-ups in a ten-year period. Finding a lab like this is not a matter of luck.

You can avoid trial and error by asking local professional photographers the name of their favorite lab. Since photographers' income is in many ways dependent on the quality of their lab, they have probably researched all the possibilities. If you find a consensus, that's the lab to go to, film in hand.

In smaller communities, don't be surprised if that lab is at some distance, often the closest city with a substantial population. I am living at the moment in a city of 55,000, where most of the pros send their film off to a lab in a city (population 500,000) 60 miles away. There is a convenient daily drop-off or pickup at a local camera store. The disadvantage is the twenty-four-hour wait before seeing your film.

To many pros, this is not a problem because of their familiarity with their current film stock/processing combination and because they have the experience to plan ahead to meet the lab's schedule. If you are on a learning curve, it's best to see the film as soon as possible, while your memory is relatively fresh. Since it may also be horribly inconvenient to keep your lighting in place for days, using a local lab of less than stellar reputation may be a necessary compromise. If you can afford it, also send a "test" roll of film to the slower but better lab. You may be able to use the better lab the next time and you will have direct personal experience of the quality of their work.

If you live out in the boonies, your only option may be to mail your film to another part of the country to be processed. The turnaround time will be at least a week (unless you are willing to absorb the cost of an overnight or two-day delivery service). In exchange for the time disadvantage, you can use the best labs in the country, often at great discounts. In addition, many film manufacturers sell their film with their own processing, or sell the processing services separately. This film/processing combination is heavily discounted by mail-order firms.

Your choice of film may restrict you to a small number of labs throughout the world. Kodachrome is an excellent and popular film that requires very expensive processing equipment due to the complexity of the process itself. This equipment costs millions, making it prohibitive to all but the largest photo operations. Unless you live in a major metropolitan area, expect to wait about a week for this film to be processed and returned to you.

The Universal Process
ONE SIZE FITS ALL

For the moment, E-6 (or its equivalent) is the most common process for transparency film around the world. The equipment required for professional quality E-6 processing is relatively inexpensive ($2,500-$100,000). There is even an amateur E-6 process to use with basic film tanks at home, although quality control would be more a matter of luck than skill. Temperature must be accurately controlled to within a quarter of a degree. The chemical condition of each step must be carefully monitored, as must the whole line of steps together, usually by processing special film strips provided by the manufacturer. A good lab will chart the results and have them available for your inspection.

Pertinent Questions to Ask Your Lab

1. *Do they process your film "in house"?* Every time your film is handled is an opportunity for it to get lost or damaged.
2. *What is the cut-off time for each run?* Only the largest labs process film continuously. Many have only one or two runs a day. It would be terrible to miss one run and have to wait an additional day. If they start early in the day, see if there is a night-drop slot.
3. *Are the control strips run before or during the processing run?* High-volume, high-quality labs run a monitor control strip first thing in the morning before any film is processed. If the results are not up to spec, they adjust and run another control strip as necessary to bring the processing line into balance and then process your film. It's nice not being the guinea pig.
4. *Does the lab push and pull processing?* Most labs can alter the first developer to slightly increase or decrease the effective film speed. This can be very useful if you have a lot of film already shot and the first roll that was sent in as a test comes back a little light or a little dark. Some labs can adjust the processing in very small increments: one-quarter stop adjustments allow for very fine tuning.

   Changing the film speed also changes the color balance. With E-6, *pushing* film by increased processing times will give the film a *warmer tone*; pulling film by decreased processing gives the film a *cooler tone*. The more you push or pull, the more the color shift. The lab will usually charge up to 50 percent more to do this "custom" work.
5. *Do you qualify for a discount?* Many labs give discounts to students, senior citizens, and state employees. You

won't know unless you ask. Some labs in New York City will give you a 25 percent discount if you pay in advance (more if you pay cold cash). If a group of you are turning in film at the same time, you might ask for a quantity discount. Be creative and negotiate.

6. *Does the lab test the films that it sells?* If the lab stocks film that it has tested and is satisfied with the results, in the scheme of things it probably is a pretty good film batch. Manufacturers make different production runs for each film. Each run is assigned an emulsion number for identification, which is printed on each package of film. If you buy film at different times but from the same emulsion run, the film characteristics will be exactly the same. Labs usually charge list price or more for this service. When you don't have time to test or reshoot, it may be worth every penny. I use the lab's films when I want to compare the results with an emulsion (from another much cheaper source) I want to buy. There are some subtle differences between emulsions (professional films will give you an actual film speed plus a filter correction if needed) and there have been and always will be some bad emulsions floating around out there. I save a few sheets or rolls so that I can actually shoot tests on a number of emulsions and have a base line for comparison. This may not make sense for you, but it's good to know how the pros do it.

What to Do While Waiting for the Film to Be Processed

In the big city, I could get my film back in two to three hours. This gave me enough time to clean up the usual mess I make when working, organize what I was going to do when the test film came back, eat a snack, and take a nap.

If the film won't get back until the next day, leave everything in place so that you won't have to repeat the work and you can be assured that your next shots will duplicate your previous efforts. If you can't block out all the light, wait until it's dark again to keep everything consistent.

If you have to send your film off to a lab faraway and you need to move the equipment to continue with your other work, follow this procedure: carefully mark the light stand's position on the floor with a piece of tape at each leg and then move the whole light stand out of the way without breaking it down any further; mark the position of the tripod in a similar fashion (you may want to remove the camera for security purposes) and put it next to the other stands. Also, remember to put your film stock in the refrigerator.

These measures will allow you to reposition the lights and tripod easily and with accuracy. Break the equipment down completely only after your session is completed. If you are going to use this same area to photograph similar work in the future, why not leave these marks on the floor? This will dramatically reduce set-up time on your next shoot.

3
Paintings, Drawings, Other Flat Artwork

Life in the Flat Lane

The information described in this chapter will provide the foundation for all the photographic lighting techniques used in this book. The lighting required to photograph flat art is simple, basic, and incredibly useful to artists of all persuasions. Read and understand this chapter before moving into the section that specifically describes photography for other media. For those who work primarily in two-dimensions, the major goal is to achieve accurate representation in the photographs of the colors as they appear in the artwork. Anyone who has already tried to do this will know how difficult and elusive it can be. Since the lighting techniques described in this chapter are quite straightforward, the challenge will be to transfer your already fine color discrimination skills into photographic realities.

Lighting and Lighting Equipment
Don't Get Caught Out in the Studio Without Your Umbrellas

Most of the time we need to have smooth, even lighting to photograph a piece of flat art. To achieve this you need to add some diffusion to the lighting to eliminate any areas of glaring

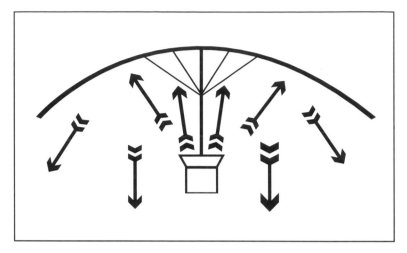

Figure 3.1A. Bounce umbrella.

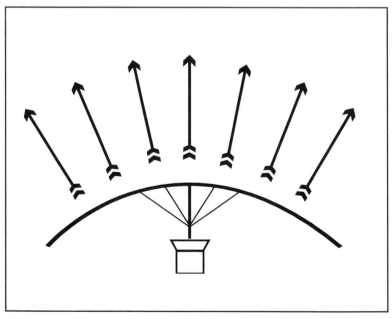

Figure 3.1B. Shoot-through umbrella.

brightness, or "hot spots," caused by the focusing of the light's reflectors. This is accomplished by using either white plexiglass filters that snap onto the reflector, or with an umbrella that is attached to the base of the lamp. Umbrellas can be either shoot-through or bounce types (see figure 3.1).

The bounce type can have a matte white or silver mylar liner, which produces a brighter, more directed light because the mylar surface is quite shiny, almost mirrorlike. The mylar-lined umbrellas will be much more difficult to work with unless the artwork being photographed is very matte, like some watercolors.

I work mostly with the shoot-through 40-inch umbrellas since they can also be used in the bounce mode. Because of their construction, bounce umbrellas can never be used as a shoot-through. The only penalty is a slight loss in light output when going from shoot-through to bounce. In most circumstances, it is preferable to use the shoot-through method because you can place the lighting closer to the art object. The bounce mode is useful when shooting large artwork in small spaces because it allows close positioning into corner areas.

The umbrellas have a larger diameter than the snap-on dif-fusers and therefore spread the light over a larger area, enabling you to photograph larger works of art. You will lose from one-half to one full stop of light with most umbrellas and diffusers. According to the size of umbrella or diffuser used, you will need either two or four lights; larger paintings may need more.

I know a painter of large, semimatte canvases who uses from twelve to sixteen clamp-on reflectors and no diffusion. He places one homemade wooden stand on each side (fashioned like a very tall coatrack) with as many lamps as he needs. In this arrangement the light is not spread evenly edge to edge, so to add sufficient light to the center of the painting he hooks several clamp lights to the sprinkler system on the studio ceiling (this may violate fire codes in certain locales, but, in any event, it must be done with great caution since these lights generate enough heat to cause the sprinklers to open). It takes

Figure 3.2. This two-light copy setup with shoot-through umbrellas was deliberately underexposed to make the lighting effect more apparent on the white walls.

Figure 3.3. This four-light copy setup with shoot-through umbrellas was also deliberately underexposed.

him forever to set up and spread the light evenly, but it works for him. The rest of the time he replaces the photo lamps with ordinary light bulbs to work on his paintings.

This method works well for very large works of art, but be prepared to use *exponentially* larger numbers of lights as the painting's size increases beyond 12 feet horizontally (the limit in most cases for a four-light setup). It is considerably easier and preferable to shoot these paintings at an installation in a gallery or museum where large spaces and lighting resources are available (see chapter 7, page 157).

Look at figures 3.2 and 3.3, showing typical two- and four-light setups and the arcs of light they produce. If the artwork is larger than the diameter of the umbrella, position a light in each corner to produce the most even lighting. It's a pretty good idea to start with the largest piece you want photograph. If you created good lighting for the largest, everything smaller will work out just fine.

Begin by setting up the lights without the umbrellas or diffusion material. This will produce obvious "hot spots" at the point of focus of each reflector. Figures 3.4 and 3.5 are deliberately underexposed to accentuate this lighting effect. If you space these "hot spots" evenly throughout the work area, the addition of the umbrellas will spread and soften the light to produce beautiful, smooth photographic results. Overlapping or combining any of these hot spots will produce an obvious unevenness on all but the most matte of surfaces, even with umbrellas.

Preparing Your Work Area
Getting a Clean Start

I generally like working on a freshly painted white wall for all sorts of reasons. It provides a clean and even background; it fills in all the nail holes that may mar an otherwise perfect photo; and it's easier to see the effects of the lighting or color balance on a white surface. Fifteen minutes spent with a paint roller is all the prep time needed for most jobs, and you've created a bright spot in your studio.

Figure 3.4. A deliberately under-exposed two-light copy setup, which shows the unevenness of light when not using umbrellas.

And don't just pick any "white" paint. Choose a white that is as neutral as possible in good daylight conditions. A few paint manufacturers even produce a "photographer's white" or a "museum white" that have specific lot numbers so that the paint can be perfectly matched. These paints are a bit more expensive but will provide a good baseline reference.

With the wall painted and the lights roughly in position, route all the cables from the lighting

Figure 3.5. This two-light setup shows the umbrellas in the bounce position.

Figure 3.6. It is best to alternate a two-light copy setup when not using a wall.

equipment clear of any walkway to the artwork and especially away from the camera position. Having a few heavy-duty extension cords (with multiple three-prong sockets) on hand will usually do the trick. If cables must be in a walking area, use highly visible tape to secure them. It is easy to trip over loose cables, especially in dimly lit areas, with potentially disastrous results. Imagine tripping over a power cord connected to a tungsten lamp, causing the light and its stand to fall through the painting you have been working on for two years, and starting a fire burning. It can and does happen, so be careful.

Small Paintings, Watercolors, and Drawings
How Not to Nail Yourself to the Wall

I have a handy two-light variation of the previous section's setup for photographing smaller flat work, especially if it is unframed and you can't tack or tape it to the wall. I use the same two-light setup procedures described in the previous section but instead of a wall, I use a flat surface at a 25- to 35-degree angle from the floor so that the artwork won't slip easily (see figure 3.6). I adjust the height of this platform so that the camera is in a comfortable working position. I use a fresh piece of matte board for the surface, which provides the same bright white background. If you buy a board that is black on one side and white on the other, you have the option to flip it over and make black borders for your artwork after you have made your test shot and corrections.

Setting Up the Camera
Three Legs Are Better Than Two

It's time to pull out your favorite camera and put it on a tripod. Do whatever you have to do to get a tripod, because the work will be easier, sharper, and more consistent. Leave yourself room to maneuver your tripod between the lights and also have easy access to the artwork for any adjustments or replacement.

Adjust the height of the camera to approximately the middle of the artwork and adjust the image size by moving the camera until the artwork nearly fills the viewfinder, leaving only a small border on each side. Assuming that we are working with a rectangle or square, carefully check to see that each border is parallel and uniform. If you have done this correctly, the camera's film plane and that of the artwork will be perfectly matched and the image will not be distorted.

Correcting Perspective Problems
Playing All the Angles

Getting rectilinear artwork perfectly "square" (all sides parallel and all corners 90 degrees) can be a real problem. Unless the camera is perfectly positioned, one or more sides of the art will be askew. This effect is exaggerated whenever normal- or short-focal-length lenses are used. The shorter the focal length, the more the image changes with an equal amount of camera movement. Any moderate telephoto (85–135mm) makes squaring the image in the viewfinder easier because it naturally flattens the perspective and decreases the angle of change as you wiggle the camera around trying to make the image square up. The longer focal length also provides more distance to the subject and easier access to the artwork.

Some cameras have interchangeable viewfinder *screens* making it possible to pop one in that has a rectilinear grid pattern (see figure 3.7). Though they only cost from $12–$30, these are often worth their weight in gold because they make it readily apparent if the image is "square."

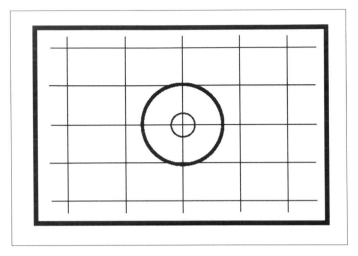

Figure 3.7. A grid viewfinder screen is a useful accessory for accurate positioning and "squaring." Most are inexpensive and can be easily installed. If your camera does not have interchangeable viewfinder screens, you can often have one permanently installed by the camera factory or repair shop at a somewhat higher cost.

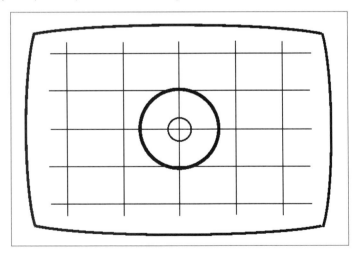

Figure 3.8. Typical view through a camera viewfinder. The sides appear bowed due to distortions of the pentaprism and viewing eyepiece. A larger pentaprism and better corrected eyepiece can eliminate the bowing, but would make the camera larger, heavier, and more expensive.

Most camera viewfinders actually bow out a bit at the extreme edge of the frame (see figure 3.8) and are not centered either vertically or laterally. To check your viewfinder's accuracy, center your artwork carefully in the viewfinder and then note the difference in the image position on your negative or unmounted transparency. There can be quite a difference! Try to assess the disparity between what the viewfinder shows you and what ends up on the film, and make allowances for it the next time you frame a shot.

If you are still having a problem getting the image square, even with long lenses and a grid screen, relax. You might just be suffering from the "forest for the trees" syndrome. Walk away and do whatever you do to release the tension. Then go back five feet behind the camera and check to see if it is indeed centered vertically and horizontally on the artwork. Chances are that it is not, so move the tripod and start over. If it is centered, grab any square and check that what you are photographing does indeed have square corners and is not warped in any way. Often times the larger stretched or framed pieces are most prone to warping, which will be further exaggerated if the wall it is mounted on is not perfectly flat. If it is not square for whatever reason, just do the best you can. Try using an even longer lens if available and space allows. The only way to correct these image distortions requires a view camera (chapter 8, page 201).

Taking Light Meter Readings
Getting Right with Light, Part II

After the image is "squared" in your viewfinder, take a hand-held *incident light meter* and move it around the surface of your artwork without blocking any light with your body. If the readings at the center *and* each corner are all within one-half an f-stop of each other, you are ready to move on to the next step. If any reading vary greater than one-half of a stop, move each light closer to or farther from the artwork until you have everything within the one-half an f-stop range. Remember that bulbs, flashtubes, or reflectors age with use and their light will begin to diminish. It's not uncommon to have to move each light vertically or horizontally a bit to create even lighting. When things look too askew it's time for new bulbs or other related equipment (see the lighting section in chapter 1).

If you only have your *in-camera meter* and want to be precise, take your camera off the tripod and remove your artwork. At close range, measure the intended work area to see if it falls within the same one-half f-stop tolerance and adjust as necessary. *Do not use this meter reading for your test or actual shot.* The meter inside your camera is measuring the light *reflected* from your work surface and assumes a "normal" subject of 18 percent neutral gray. If you follow this meter reading blindly, your white walls would reproduce as gray in your shot and everything would appear darker than normal. You need to compensate by opening up 2 to 2½ f-stops to get into the ballpark. The advantage of an incident light meter is that it reads the light *falling onto* your work area and automatically adjusts the exposure into a workable range.

For a quicker but less precise method, you can use your in-camera meter (even on automatic) for overall exposure settings as you do in everyday situations if your artwork is not predominantly white or black. If your art is much darker than 18 percent gray you must decrease the exposure a bit by using a smaller aperture. If your art is lighter than photographic gray you must increase the exposure by using a larger aperture. To be precise, refer to figure 1.2. Pick the zone that best represents the overall light value, and increase the exposure one stop for every zone darker than the middle zone (zone IV). If the art is mostly zone II values, you will need to increase your exposure by two stops. Conversely, if the art is mostly zone VI values, decrease the exposure by two stops. Automatic camera owners need to be in the "manual" mode to be able to do this. Check your camera's manual for instructions. With a little experience you will be able to estimate with great accuracy without referring to the zone scale.

Shooting Art Behind Glass
Where Did All Those Reflections Come From?

It is always best to remove glass before shooting any artwork. The glass may not be of good quality and any dirt on either side of it is likely to show up in the photo, as will reflections of you and the camera. But there have been many occasions when I have been unable (or unwilling to take the responsibility) to remove the glass. Reflections can also happen with smooth, shiny, and dark oil paintings. You shouldn't change your style if you create surfaces that are shiny, slick, and reflective and therefore more difficult to photograph; but you should make your life easier and remove glass whenever possible.

To deal with the reflections in the glass (or the actual painted surface), you just need to get the camera and lights into the correct position. With the exposure already figured out, hang a black backdrop parallel to the wall on which the art is hanging and just in front of the camera lens (see figure 3.9). The back-

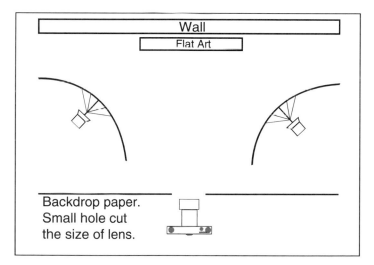

Figure 3.9. Top view of camera and backdrop position for shooting highly reflective flat art or art behind glass.

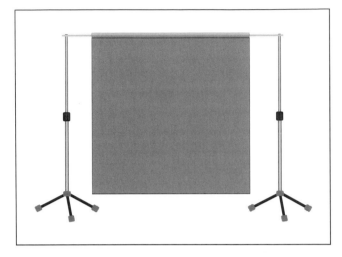

Figure 3.10. Portable backdrop stand.

drop has to be big enough, both top to bottom and edge to edge, to reflect a featureless black onto the glass. There will be no reflected objects in the room to show up on the glass (or painted) surface.

When you are sure that all reflections are masked, cut a hole just large enough for the lens to stick through and double-check your image for reflections through the viewfinder. Black backdrop paper come in rolls that are 12 yards long and 54 or 108 inches wide. You may be able hang a piece of the backdrop roll from the ceiling with duct or gaffer's tape, but this arrangement is hard to adjust or move.

I use a set of portable backdrop stands (see figure 3.10) and a 108-inch roll. When it is time to cut the camera hole I pull down the backdrop or "seamless" until it reaches the ground and rolls up naturally for an additional 3 to 4 feet. I finish the shot and simply roll the seamless back up and out of my way. I then have easy access to set up the next shot and pull down the seamless again, if needed. At the end of the shoot, I roll the seamless up tightly, and tape it in several spots so that it doesn't develop creases or waves. I also label it as having a camera hole and will use it over and over.

This is the easiest and least expensive way to eliminate glass and other surface reflections. The stands can be rented (or you may come up with your own homemade design), but you must buy the paper.

A *polarizing filter* attached to the lens may eliminate enough of the reflections to make a suitable photo in special situations. This filter actually consists of two light gray filters that work in combination, and that are stacked on top of each other. Rotating the outer filter will constantly vary the effect and can reduce or eliminate reflections depending on the angle to the lens axis. This "polarization" is most effective whenever at a 90-degree angle from the light source and gradates as it approaches the lens axis. Most of the time our lighting is only 45 degrees off axis. My experience has been that some reflections do remain if filtered this way. When using this filter, you will need to add one to two stops more exposure depending on the amount of polarization.

The most appropriate method of polarization for removing glass reflections is to filter the light source. Each light would need its own single filter polarizer, which would be rotated to act in combination with all the other filters to eliminate reflections. The lights should be set at a 90-degree angle to each other in relation to the lens axis for optimum results. These filters are substantially more expensive because they are larger and need to be heat-resistant.

Keeping Track of Your Efforts
How to Avoid Being Derailed

The real trick to achieving professional consistency is to write everything down as you work! Relying on your memory alone is like playing Russian roulette, and can result in costly errors. Record every exposure setting and light meter reading. I always write my exposure notes on a sticky label and put it right on the camera. This gives me a quick reference for the proper exposure whenever I am about to shoot. When you get your film back, determine what worked and what didn't and write that down, too (we'll get into corrections later). Once you have the desired results, you can even mark the position of your camera and light stands on your studio floor. I make small *X*s with white or black tape, whatever shows up best. This considerably reduces set-up time at your next shoot and, if you are very careful, you won't need to do a test shot.

Final Checks and Common Errors

After you have set up the lights properly, arrived at your exposure solution (and written it down), and accurately centered your artwork in the viewfinder, you can finally begin exposing the film. But beware: this is the point when the most mistakes are made, both by amateurs and professionals. It may seem obvious, but do you have the right (or any) film in your camera? And is it loaded properly? All but a few cameras have the film rewind knob readily visible. If you take up the film slack in its canister by winding gently in the direction of the rewind arrow until it is snug, the knob will spin opposite the arrow every time you advance the film. I make this even more obvious by leaving the rewind crank in its up position (see figure 3.11).

Another common mistake is not setting the film speed correctly on your built-in or handheld meter. Unless you have the Polaroid equipment to check your exposure, correct indexing of film speed is the only way to assure yourself controllable results.

Now is the time for all the final checks. Tighten down all the controls on your tripod and make sure your camera is firmly attached. Check carefully for any signs of glare from your lighting on your art—being especially careful if the artwork's finish is high gloss; it will be easier if you have eliminated all ambient light by closing all doors, windows, and blinds. Remember that the angle of incidence equals the angle of reflectance (see figure 3.12). Peering just over the top of your camera (looking *through* the camera may not work because everything will appear a bit dimmer) inspect each corner of your art piece for any unwanted hot spots. These hot spots will be even more

Figure 3.11. The rewind crank (on the top left of this 35mm camera seen from behind) is extended for easy recognition of the film transporting through the camera.

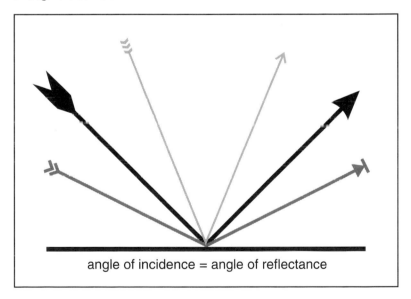

angle of incidence = angle of reflectance

Figure 3.12. Light will bounce off a highly reflective surface at a similar angle to that which it came in on, much like the action of a bouncing basketball or a bank shot in billiards. Matte surfaces scatter these light reflections over a great range of angles, which diminishes the intensity of the reflection but does not totally eliminate it. Exercise the same care on matte and semimatte artwork to eliminate unwanted glare.

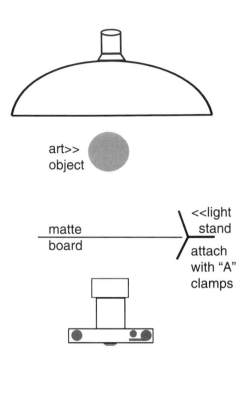

art>>
object

matte
board

<<light
stand

attach
with "A"
clamps

Figure 3.13A. Block the lens from the direct light from light sources to eliminate potential lens flare. From the art object position, look back at your lens for any reflection of light sources. If you see any part of the light bank, umbrella, or light bulb, position a card close to the lens just enough to block it out. If your lighting is very close to the art, you may not be able to block all the direct light from hitting the lens. You will need a card on both sides of the lens when using a copy setup for flat artwork.

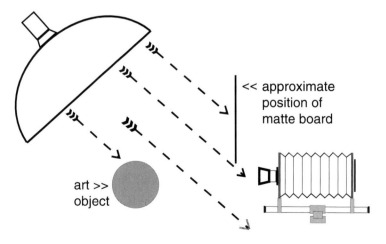

<< approximate
position of
matte board

art >>
object

Figure 3.13B. Side view of figure 3.13A.

evident on film and are usually very distracting. Moving the lighting farther away or changing the angle of the lighting in relation to the art will solve this problem.

The next important step is to make certain that your lighting is not shining directly into your lens. With your back to the art-work, try to position your head exactly on the lens axis and look at your lens surface. If you see a reflection of any lighting on the front element, now is the time to block this out with a lens shade or piece of matte board (see figure 3.13A and B). This unwanted stray light may bounce around the lens elements and produce areas of lower contrast and color saturation, giving a somewhat "ghostlike" appearance.

Take another quick look through the viewfinder to make sure everything is where it's supposed to be, and check to make sure the aperture and shutter speed are properly set. Then you will be finally ready to take your first picture! The rest of the shots should go quickly after this, and these last checks should only take 30 seconds, tops (providing nothing else has moved or fallen). Compared to the time you'd spend doing reshoots, to say nothing of the expense, these few seconds are well spent.

One final note about exposing your film. A cable release will reduce camera vibration and produce sharper results because you are not actually touching or pushing on the camera itself. It is still necessary to squeeze the plunger slowly. Another trick is to set the camera's self-timer (consult your camera's user's man-ual) and let the camera take the shot. It is important that you be stationary, too, when releasing the shutter by cable or timer, to ensure the sharpest results. The slower the shutter speed, the more important it is to eliminate as much vibration as possible. So turn down the stereo, put the dog in the next room, make anyone else present sit down or stand still, breathe deeply and hold your breath, listen and feel for any vibration and then release the shutter if everything is "quiet."

Exposures longer than 1/30th of a second (1/15th, 1/8th, 1/4th, and so on) require even more attention when using an SLR. The mirror that allows you to see the image in the viewfinder swings up during exposure and hits its stop in about one-tenth of a second, producing image-degrading vibration during longer exposures. If your camera has the capability, lock the mirror into the up position before the exposure. Some cameras do this automatically when the self-timer is used and this is quite convenient. Just make sure nothing else moves until after the exposure.

The All-Important Exposure Bracket

Taking test shots is a wise idea since they will establish the proper exposure for accuracy. It's best to make three different exposures when testing transparency films. Start with your normal exposure, followed by one a half-stop lighter and then one a half-stop darker than normal. This procedure is called *bracketing*. For example, if the normal exposure is 1/60th at f8, the three exposures would be f8, then halfway between f5.6 and f8, then halfway between f8 and f11. Most lenses have a click-stop you can feel at each f-stop and each one-half f-stop. If yours doesn't, carefully position the indicator halfway between the stops.

Bracketing is an important tool to help you arrive at the perfectly exposed transparency. If the exposure meter, the camera shutter speed, the actual film speed, and the quality of the processing are all perfect, then, like Goldilocks, one exposure will be too light, one too dark, and one just right.

With experience and careful notes, you can keep all these variables under control and hit the mark almost every time. It may happen that a lighter exposure may produce a more pleasing photographic result, especially if the artwork is very dark. Or, perhaps, you may choose a slightly darker exposure to make the colors more saturated and pleasing to the eye. Make the appropriate choice from your test shots and write that down, too. Then go back and shoot a few more frames so that you'll have extra copies.

To be able to shoot exposure brackets, it is usually necessary to place an automatic camera into its manual mode of operation. However, a few automatic cameras have a convenient dial that allows setting specific amounts of under- or overexposure. Some high-end models can even be programmed to automatically shoot brackets whenever the shutter is released. Carefully check your camera's instruction booklet for any of these features and for manual-mode operation.

It's always good practice to use the following checklist before shooting each new piece of artwork:

Final Checklist for Flat Artwork

1. Complete lighting and tape cords down or out of way.
2. Keep work area free of adverse external or ambient light.
3. Check for proper setting of film speed on light meter.
4. Set aperture and f-stop for correct exposure solution and write it down!
5. Center and "square" image in the viewfinder.
6. Focus critically and inspect image for unwanted glare and/or reflections.
7. Tighten all locks on tripod head, legs, and camera attachment.
8. Check for unwanted glare on lens.
9. Make sure the correct film is properly loaded and transporting through the camera.
10. Eliminate as much vibration as possible.
11. Make one-half f-stop exposure bracket.
12. Check viewfinder to see if image has moved.
13. Set up next shot and repeat.

Detail Shots

Before you remove one piece of art and replace it with the next, consider shooting an interesting detail shot of a small section of your work. The larger the art piece the more important detail shots are since intricate details tend to disappear when the original is reduced in size (if the original is 4×6 feet and you are doing a 35mm slide at $1 \times 1\frac{1}{2}$ inches you have reduced the image by a factor of forty-eight). All you need to do in most instances is bring the camera in a little closer to the piece.

Moderate telephoto lenses (85mm–135mm) will give you about one-seventh life-size reproduction on film at their closest focus setting. You can easily record a 7 × 10-inch section of your artwork. At reproduction ratios greater than one-tenth life-size, you must compensate with additional exposure unless you are relying solely on your built-in meter. Our example of one-seventh life-size reproduction requires an additional three-eighths f-stop larger than the one suggested by a handheld meter.

It may take several detail shots to tell the whole story about one painting, so do as many as you need to provide a complete representation of the piece. Additionally, you want to emphasize the surface texture or paint strokes in separate shots. Accomplish this by turning off the light(s) farthest away from the detail. More pronounced shadows will appear that enhance the three-dimensional effect. Be sure to take a new meter reading after getting the effect you want.

Extreme close-ups will be covered in chapter 6, page 127. Refer to that section if want to explore the possibilities if getting *really* close. Special equipment will be needed.

4

Three-Dimensional Art

How to Keep It from Going Flat

Although I enjoy photographing all forms of artwork, I get the most professional satisfaction from working with three-dimensional objects. Unlike the photography of painting, where we strive to ensure a factual representation, *photos of objects are more interpretive.* There are dozens of choices to be made that will determine the feeling and effectiveness of the final photo.

If you approach photographing objects as a participatory endeavor, half the battle is over. The more actively you involve your senses and intellect, the better you can translate your three-dimensional object into a two-dimensional photograph. Think of your photograph as a whole new creation with your object as the star of the show. Make the photo an extension of your creative powers.

Making a photo of three-dimensional art demands a good deal of observation and adjustment. The tools and effects we have to work with should already be familiar to you as an artist: light and shade, perspective and background. You just need to understand how to manipulate each of these accordingly.

Lighting
What You Need to Ignite Your Career

Native Americans used to call early photographers shadow catchers, a very perceptive interpretation of a photographic print. From all the light in the world, the photographer's magical apparatus captured only shadows and darkness.

For the purpose of photographing artwork, think of yourself as throwing light instead of catching shadows. Like talented magicians, we want to create certain illusions by throwing artificial light at something and making it seem totally "natural." Your audience is willing to buy into the illusion, having been bombarded with millions of contrived images that they accept as "reality."

The first illusion is to create a natural-looking light. For those of us in the middle latitudes, the light we experience outside during most of the day is from above and at a 45- to 60-degree angle to the horizon. This "natural light" is our common standard, so we hardly notice it at all.

However, we do notice when the light changes. For example, at sunset the shadows are longer and deeper and there is a distinct shift in color cast. Sunset creates an emotional and instinctive response in most human beings: it's time to start thinking about finding some food and a safe place for the night.

This is not the response you want elicit with your photograph. If you want your object to really stand out on its own, you don't want to notice the lighting at all! The light still has to be there—you just don't want it to be intrusive. Re-creating a natural feeling to your light makes it virtually disappear.

We make this light in the studio by creating a broad light source at a 45- to 60-degree angle, mimicking the sky and sun at midday. For photomechanical purposes, we want to add a thin, high overcast to the sky to lighten the intensity of the shadows. To complete our illusion, we make the light source come from behind (backlighting) to help separate the various planes of your three-dimensional object in our two-dimensional image (see figure 4.1). Sounds simple, and it is. We can't expect this

Figure 4.1. Ceramic water vessel, George E. Ohr, c.1900, 7"h. The highlight produced by backlighting helps separate the object from the background. This is especially important if the colors or tonalities of both are similar.

type of lighting to be used for everything, but it does form the basic photographic lighting that we can build upon and adapt whenever necessary.

Perspective
Spherical to Flat and Back

Perspective is controlled by the *focal length of the lens* and *camera positioning*. Using a classic "portrait" lens (85mm to 105mm on 35mm cameras) produces a "natural" perspective; the photographic result is neither flattened nor exaggerated as it could be with longer telephotos or any wide-angle lens. Remember, the goal is to create an interpretive but factual representation of your art. An 85mm to 105mm lens will virtually guarantee your art will appear the same photographically as it does in person.

Normal lenses, around 50mm in focal length, require much more care whenever used, specifically when focused closer than 4 feet (this does not apply to extreme close-up, covered in chapter 6, or for any flat surface that is photographed square on). The art object may look longer, rounder, or taller than it really is. Although these distortions may be quite subtle, it may

Figure 4.2A, B. Clay sculpture, Arnonson, 1975. I used an 85mm lens and a low camera position to make these photos. The back of the bottle crate appears slightly smaller in the photograph because it is farther away (about 6 feet) from the camera than is the crate's front (about 4 feet). To make the same size image with a 24mm wide-angle lens, the camera would need to be positioned much closer to the front of the art object (about 1 foot). The back of the object, about 3 feet away, appears much smaller than the front of the object because it is three times the distance away. If we used a 180mm lens, the front of the object would be about 8 feet away, the back about 10 feet away. This would minimize the difference in size between the front and back of the art object, but would make the art appear extremely foreshortened. (See figure 1.5.)

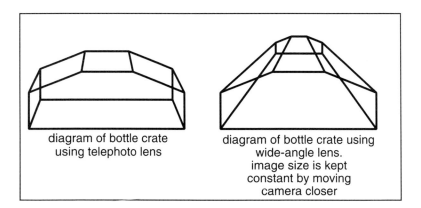

diagram of bottle crate
using telephoto lens

diagram of bottle crate using
wide-angle lens.
image size is kept
constant by moving
camera closer

Figure 4.2C. An illustration of Figures 4.2A and 4.2B showing the principle of convergence.

create a shocking difference to someone who looked at the photo first and then later saw the object in person.

You should avoid using wide-angle lenses at all costs because they will create obvious distortions of the objects you are photographing. Another disadvantage that makes them much less useful in photo setup is that because wide-angle lenses see a larger viewing field, the lighting must be farther away from the object and a much larger background surface is required.

We can also control perspective by choosing the camera's placement in relation to the art object. A camera positioned to look down at a 20- to 45-degree angle adds to the illusion of depth in the photo front to back (since we can see more of the top of the object) but somewhat foreshortens the object vertically. The higher the camera's position in relation to the horizon, the more pronounced the foreshortening and the greater the image distortion will be since objects diminish in size in ratio to their distance from the camera. A shorter lens will exaggerate this diminishing effect; a longer lens will the flatten the perspective and reduce the diminishing effect (see figure 4.2). Unless your artwork has strong, straight verticals, elevating the camera position from the horizon is hardly noticed and resembles the usual viewing angle in real life.

Another rule to keep in mind is that looking up at an object makes it appear both larger and taller than it really is (a common advertising trick) and again distorts any vertical line that is not dead center. These lines will appear closer together toward the center of the frame the farther away they are from the camera. The more rapidly this happens, the farther away it appears as the vertical lines converge, or come together. With the camera positioned well below the horizon and using a wide-angle lens, this illusion can be greatly amplified.

For owners of some 35mm cameras, interchangeable viewfinder screens are available with an engraved grid pattern (see figure 3.7, page 40). This can be very useful aid in determining exactly how far off vertical any line is throughout the frame since there are usually several reference lines. It may be impossible to eliminate all the image distortions discussed above, no

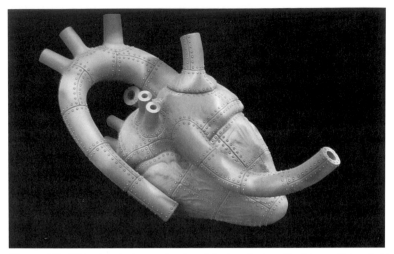

Figure 4.3. Objects photographed on black velvet or flocking will produce no shadows on the background surface. Since shadows help the viewer orient the photograph correctly, be sure to include an "up" indication or other reference to ensure that the image is properly viewed.

matter where your 35mm camera is placed or what lens you use. Image distortions are typically controlled optical adjustments available on a 4 × 5 or similar cameras (see chapter 8).

Backgrounds
Out of Obscurity and into the Forefront

Unless you want your object to appear to be floating in space (see figure 4.3), a surface or background of some sort is needed for visual support and a sense of gravity. A plain roll of backdrop paper (or any solid-color surface for smaller objects) is quite effective and visually pleasing. By controlling the light to create a "fall-off" (going from light to dark) in the distance, an illusion of depth is preserved (see figures 4.4A and 4.4B). Creating depth on the surface the object is sitting on adds interest to the photo without destroying the photo's simplicity. This helps you enhance the art without distracting the viewer.

A background does not need to be completely featureless (see figure 4.5) as long as it doesn't make the photograph look

Figure 4.4A. Limited-edition porcelain for Artes Magnus by Arman. "Accumulation, As in the Sink I," 1990. Contrast this with figure 4.4B. These two art pieces are very similar at first glance. A different background was used for each to let the viewer easily realize that these were two, distinct photographs.

Figure 4.4B. "Accumulation, As in the Sink II," 1990 (on black background).

too "busy"—with too many things happening at once. Every added element must play a supportive role to the focus of your photo—your art.

You may want to combine a surface with a background. Spend as much time as you want creating your backgrounds and surfaces with the caveat of the preceding paragraph in mind; but remember you are showing people your art, not your set-building capabilities.

Rolls of backdrop paper are available in a wide range of colors and shades, enabling you to tailor a color to the object you are shooting. These rolls are either 54 or 109 inches wide and 12 yards in length. When not in use, the rolls should be tightly wrapped and stored vertically to keep the paper from rippling (which may take days to smooth out on the set) when unrolled.

Figure 4.5. Ceramic by Betty Woodman. "Minoan Pillow Pitcher," 26"w, 23"h, 17"d, 1987. The background is a painted canvas I had created to use for making portraits of people. Its muted, mottled colors add extra textures to the photo's background without attracting too much attention. A background like this is best when slightly out of focus.

Later in this chapter I'll describe how to use and make backdrop holders.

Rippling of the paper on the set may be due to high humidity and pressure from the object. This rippling may never go away—in that case just cut away the damaged paper and roll out a fresh portion.

I like to use 4 × 8-inch sheets of formica as backdrops whenever possible. These are widely available at building supply shops in a variety of colors and textures. They are immune to wrinkling and rippling, and withstand heavy use without showing wear. In the long run formica may be more cost effective than paper rolls. However, their "perfect" finish can be damaged or marred by sharp edges and mishandling. Lift the art object rather than sliding it along the surface to prevent scratching the formica's surface. After a lot of use, some scratching is inevitable. Just hide them under or behind the object so that you don't see them in the photograph. When one end of the formica gets too scratched, use the other end. The scratched end will generally be out of the frame or out of focus.

The formica sheet curves easily to produce a number of gradation effects, and can be rolled into a fairly tight circle for storage or transport. The more you roll it up, however, the more the chance of damaging the surface. I store my sheets by leaning them carefully against the wall and placing something in front of them big enough to keep them from falling over. A couch or bookcase in your home would work very well.

Tabletop Photography of Small to Medium-Sized Objects
Keeping Your Art Strictly Aboveboard

Professionals refer to the photography of small objects as *tabletop photography*. This is an accurate description of the area we'll be working with in this section. A typical table (28 to 30 inches) will hold your object at a convenient height and allows you to work standing up. This also places the camera's position at about eye level, which is within the working range of reasonably priced tripods. Since many art objects of this size are meant to be displayed at table height, the perspective will be natural.

The size of the tabletop required obviously depends on the object's size. Since backdrop rolls are typically 54 inches wide, a table that is about 3 × 5 feet should work just fine. In general, larger tables are easier to work with if space and budget permits. If you don't have a large enough table, it's simple to make one. I use wooden or metal sawhorses with either a piece of plywood or a hollow door of appropriate size. I have several different leg lengths for the wooden sawhorses to provide the most comfortable working height, one that doesn't put stress on my back.

All About Reflectors
It Really Is Done with Smoke and Mirrors

Figure 4.6 is a photograph of a multiple-cast and assembled ceramic piece titled "Animal Tower" by Jack Charney of Santa Fe, New Mexico. It uses the "natural" lighting I spoke of earlier and mimics midafternoon daylight when there is a high, thin overcast (figure 4.7 shows a side view).

By using one broad, diffused light source you keep the lighting simple and create only one shadow at the base in front of the piece, much like the sun does in the middle of the after-

Figure 4.6A–D. (Clockwise from top left) Multicast assembled ceramic by Jack Charney. "Animal Tower," 12"h, 1993. This nearly black object required a white background and numerous reflector fill cards to produce a photograph with adequate and visible detail throughout. The clear, shiny glaze made this easier to accomplish. The cards need to be more precisely shaped and placed since the highlights are mirrorlike sharp reflections of the lighting elements. (See figures 4.7-4.10)

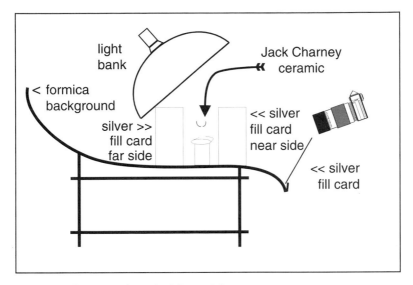

Figure 4.7 Sideview, Step A of figure 4.6 setup.

noon. This is a very heavy, deep shadow that you need to "fill in" with additional light. You could eliminate this shadow by using more lights, but these would add to the equipment expense, and generally complicate the shoot by making additional shadows in different and confusing directions.

A more controllable method is to harness some of the excess light from the main source with reflectors placed outside the frame area. Two of the three reflectors you see in figure 4.7 are pieces of matte board with silver foil on one side, and the third is an 8 × 10-inch piece of white matte board. All were positioned to bounce enough light into the shadow areas to make them light enough to appear on film with good detail. They are also positioned to emphasize surface detail and the texture of the shiny three layers of clear glaze (the underglaze is a very dark, almost black, cobalt blue). Let's look at how the finished photo was accomplished step by step.

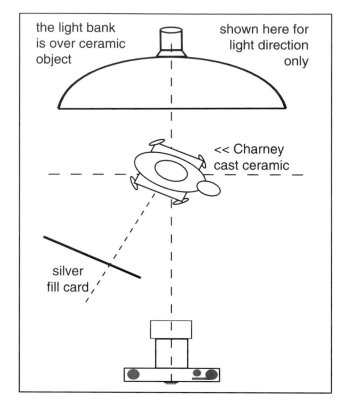

Figure 4.8. Top view, Step B.

Step A: I started with the object centered left to right and front to back beneath the main light. Note that the main light is at a 45-degree angle to the surface. Most of the light striking the object is coming from behind, creating a lighting called *back-lighting,* meaning that the object is lit from the back (figure 4.7). This lighting places a highlight around the top and edges of the object, visually separating the object from the background. This light also helps define the planes of the object from front to back, aiding the three-dimensional illusion in the final photograph. I moved the object forward and backward until I found a position where I thought the object looked its best (almost to the back edge of the light bank).

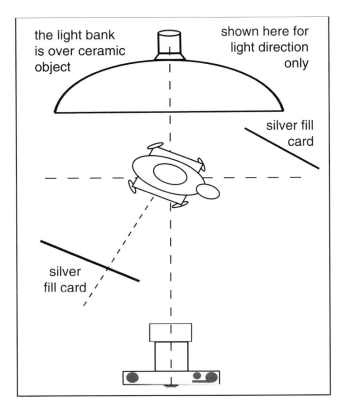

Figure 4.9. Top view, Step C.

As you can see, this light alone will not help create a very pretty or complete picture, although to the untrained eye it will probably look much better viewing it on the set than it does in this photo. The animal figures are lit enough to see most of the shapes and curves, but there are large areas of featureless dark black that need to be lightened in tone to give these areas a more complete shape in the photograph. The side of the base that most faces the camera is the largest and most distracting black hole in the photo and should be addressed first.

Step B: I added a white reflector board (16 × 30 inches) positioned about 30 degrees from the lens axis (when viewed directly from above) to *parallel* the darkest side of the object (figure 4.8). (If your object doesn't have an obvious flat side like this, it is better to start with a 45-degree angle.) This lightened the dark area, but not nearly enough. I replaced the white reflector with a silver reflector, which was used for the actual photograph. The reflected light from the silver reflector card is both stronger in intensity and more directional. Small movements, in both distance and angle, produce greater image changes than would be possible with white reflectors. In this example, I moved the reflector in as close as possible without showing it in the film frame. While looking from the camera's position, I also adjusted the reflector's vertical angle to maximize the light intensity on the vase. I propped it up against a bottle to hold it at the angle of maximum reflectance. Sometimes a piece of tape may be necessary to secure the card in place, as it was in this instance. I moved the card as close as possible to the object because I needed as much reflected light as possible. Note that the shadow areas in the animal figures are smaller and lighter, especially the side of the turtle's face.

It was also important that this reflector be tall enough to ensure that the whole face of the base was flooded with the reflection of the card. A shorter card would have left a sharply defined dark rectangle at the top of the face. The little ripple (at edge of the top of the side face) is a reflection of the bottom of the turtle that cannot be eliminated.

Step C: I introduced another 12 × 15-inch silver reflector directly opposite the first silver card and behind the object to add a bright highlight to the side of the base to the camera's right (figure 4.9). Using a white card made this area light enough, but the silver card gave this surface more apparent texture. The silver card's vertical angle had to be carefully adjusted to avoid creating a new highlight that would be too bright and overpowering.

The card is positioned just outside the frame area. On a darker surface, any card so positioned would probably cause an obvious streak of light to appear on the surface inside the frame area. Avoid this by moving the card a few more inches farther out.

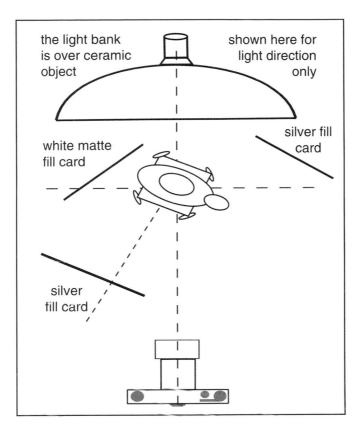

the light bank
is over ceramic
object

shown here for
light direction
only

silver fill
card

white matte
fill card

silver
fill card

Figure 4.10. Top view, Step D.

Step D: I added one more reflector to create a small but needed highlight on the hand at the left corner of the base (figure 4.10). This 8 × 10-inch reflector, too, was placed just outside the frame area but to the left. The closer the card was to the frame edge, the bigger the reflection (highlight) on this small hand. With a complicated piece like this, you must pay attention to every small detail to be completely successful in the photograph.

Because this piece was so reflective, I had to place a several other reflectors around this set, not so much to to add reflections (it did to a very minor but not apparent degree) but to block reflections from around the studio environment (light stands, camera, rolls of backdrop paper, etc). I added 30 × 40-inch pieces of white foam core one at a time all around the set, carefully checking from the camera position for any noticeable change in the object. Because the top of this piece is relatively complex, the shapes of these large cards are not apparent. If this object were a simpler sphere, for example, you would need to exercise much greater care in card placement and the shape of the reflection it creates. Be on the lookout whenever reflector cards meet at the corners or wherever they overlap because the dark lines they create might be noticeably reflected onto the spherical object.

I have photographed a few objects more than once—often years apart. There are always subtle differences between the photographs because of the subjective choices I made in each instance. Most of the time, the newer photo wasn't better than the older; it was just a different interpretation.

Choosing or Making Your Broad Light Source
Sometimes Bigger Is Better

The previous section demonstrated how a broad light source can be used to re-create a "natural" light, much like the sun and sky, for photographing three-dimensional artwork. You need to figure out a way to acquire or create such a light setup within your budget. Prices for lighting equipment on the market vary widely. Generally, the more expensive lights have higher material quality and are easier to handle. Although photographers tend to drift toward better equipment as they become more established, I have yet to meet one who hasn't made or improvised his or her own lighting.

I have made dozens of my own lights over the years either because I couldn't afford to buy them, or because there wasn't anything on the market to meet my needs. Using your ingenuity and the materials at hand, you can produce photographic results indistinguishable from those made using store-bought lighting. Read through all of the following examples to help match your needs to your pocketbook.

Lighting Option 1
Making Nothing at All—And More

Corporate and industrial location photographers don't have the luxury of time or of choosing of their own settings in much of their work. Yet they are able to produce stunning results with a few lights and reflectors, relying on making the most of the existing environment. In many architectural settings, ceilings are relatively low and white. Much location work depends on using this surface as a built-in reflector to create a broad light source from above.

For our purposes, a corner of a room with white walls and a 7-to-9-foot ceiling would be ideal for many objects. Figure 4.5 (page 60) is an example of what can be done in such an area with just two lights. The piece in figure 4.5, by Betty Woodman, was a very tricky object to shoot because of its shiny surfaces and smooth curves.

The Main Light

A single light, to the right and just behind the object, was pointed straight up at the ceiling to create a broad, "natural" light source. The light was positioned to produce moderate backlight and to minimize the shadow in front of the object. This light source will provide most of the overall illumination and is therefore called the *main light.*

Raising and lowering this light changes the effect it has on the highlight on the right side of the rounded part of the pitcher when viewed from the approximate camera position (30 degrees above the horizon); lowering the light created a broader, and therefore more diffuse light on the ceiling, which was reflected in the glaze. Raising the light made a smaller but brighter light that was more directional and created more contrasty lighting. I found that a midpoint between the two lighting extremes produced the most pleasing result in that the large

Figure 4.11A, B. Two views of Betty Woodman pillow pitcher, 1985. Compare the reflection of the main light (the almost white rectangle with very defined edges) of these two photos with the highlight created in Figure 4.5. Figure 4.11 was simpler and quicker to shoot. Figure 4.5 took much longer to set up but is more aesthetically pleasing.

highlight reflection had a very bright, almost white center that gradually disappeared into the color of the glaze, giving it an airbrushed look.

There are a number of complicated and tedious ways to light this piece with very diffuse lighting where we would not see its apparent reflection, but we would then lose the clues about the surface texture. Where it is glossy and slick, the reflections on the surface must look glossy and slick. The real trick is to place the highlight reflection in an appropriate place and create an aesthetically pleasing shape.

Figure 4.11 illustrates a different approach. It is an earlier version of another pillow pitcher shot in my studio with a 4-foot-square light source. The highlight reflection shows up as a rectangle since it is on a curve. The problem is that the rectangle has both sharply defined edges as well as a solid, uniform tone. In this instance, using the ceiling as a much larger and modulated light source produced an image that is visually much more pleasing.

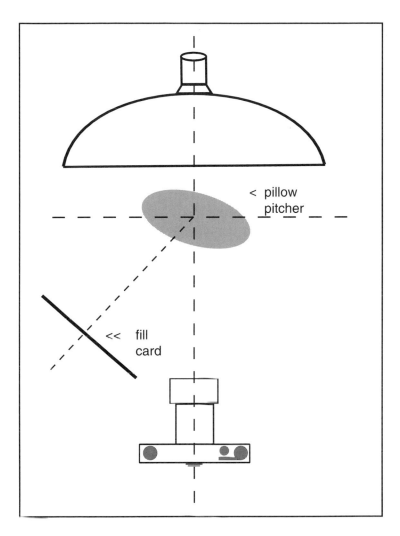

Figure 4.12. Top view of the lighting setup for figure 4.11. This illustrates a good starting position for fill-card placement.

Fill Light

Since the main light is slightly behind the art object, a significant part of the front of the piece is in shadow, producing photographic results that would be too dark in that area. Additional

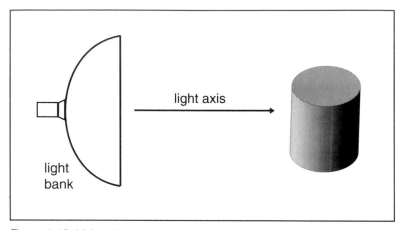

light axis

light bank

Figure 4.13. Light axis and shadows.

light is almost always needed to brighten up this shadow area (on direct axis from the light, see figure "light axis"), even though everything may appear fine to your naked eye. The first step is always to place a reflector, otherwise known as a *fill card* (since you are indeed filling in the shadows) at a 45-degree angle to an imaginary line that extends from the light through the object (see figure 4.12).

In this example, I placed a 30 × 40-inch piece of foam core just outside the frame area. The white matte surface was adjusted vertically to reflect enough light into the shadows without making them totally disappear. This size board was necessary to produce a seamless reflection in the whole width of the object. Since this ceramic object is quite smooth and reflective, shorter reflectors would leave dark gaps at each end where there is no board reflecting onto the surface. If two boards were overlapped, the seam would be readily apparent in the reflection. A silver reflector of the same size would produce hard, bright, unattractively shaped reflections. To produce the desired effect, you can also adjust the board angle as seen from above. This was not necessary for this photograph but was important in our previous example (figure 4.6, page 62), where the angle needed to be reduced to about 30 degrees.

It is important to try out a number of reflector options and combinations to see what will work best. With experience, you should be able to select the best two or three; keep these readily available for future use. Insert and take away each type of reflector a few times and carefully observe the effects, especially noting any hard-edged reflections. Experiment with different sizes and shapes. I often cut the matte board to reflect certain shapes that will follow the form of a reflective object.

At this point it is good to establish your final camera position *on a tripod.* Fill cards have a way of making unexpected "guest appearances" in the frame area. Recheck your setup thoroughly after each card insertion or adjustment.

Background Light

Refer to figure 4.5 (page 60). The pillow pitcher was placed on a small table with a white formica surface. The table was placed about 3 feet away from the wall, to which I taped a mottled painted canvas. This canvas was chosen because its colors were complementary to the colors of the object. Without additional light, this background looked okay, but it improved dramatically when another light below the table was used to add a highlight to the canvas, this is known as a *background light.* The light's round reflector created both the curved shape and the gradation in the light, an effect of the light's natural fall-off as it moves away from the reflector's angle of coverage. In this instance, the direct, raw light (directly from the lamp to the canvas) could be used because the canvas is very matte. On smoother surfaces, this same raw light would probably look smaller, mostly white, overexposed, and unappealing.

The light would need to be further diffused, or scattered, to create the smooth, pleasing gradation that figure 4.5 exhibits. Some lighting equipment has accessory white plexi disks or a variety of screen grids that snap onto the rim of the reflector to produce a range of light diffusion. If you have these accessories, try each one until you find one with the effect you desire. Because these accessories are in close proximity to the lamp, they will get hot very quickly. Wear heavy gloves when handling them, even if the light has been on a few seconds.

If you have no accessories or cannot find the effect you want, try using layers of tracing paper curved into an arc by taping them to the top and bottom of the reflector. The arc shape provides some space on the sides for ventilation. Each additional layer of paper diffuses and diminishes the output of the light a bit more. Add one layer at a time until you achieve the desired effect.

The hotter the light, the quicker the paper will age and turn brown, becoming a potential a fire hazard if left unattended for any length of time. Putting diffusion attachments (makeshift or manufactured) in front of a lamp increases the bulb temperature while decreasing, often dramatically, the lamp's useful life. Turn these lamps off whenever they are not being used.

Meter Readings
Getting Right with Light

Since figure 4.5 shows the effect of two lights aimed in different directions, it is important to know the light output ratio between them, even though it may look perfectly fine on the set. With all the lights and reflectors in position, take a meter reading of the main light with the background light turned off. Hold a handheld meter just on top of the object, point the sensor directly at the main light source (the ceiling in this case), and take a measurement. In this example, the main light metered f22.

Now turn off the main light and measure the intensity of the light coming from the background source by pointing your metering cell directly at the backdrop. In this example, the background light measured f16, or one full stop darker than the main light. Since I wanted the background just slightly darker than the foreground, this was just perfect.

If this had metered two full stops difference, I would be concerned that the background glow might disappear altogether in the photo. I would compensate by moving this light closer until there was only a one-stop difference or by using a lamp with twice the wattage (not possible in this case). Conversely, if the meter reading was equal to or higher than the reading of the main light, the background might appear too light and not sufficiently distinct in tone from the object to the point where it might be difficult to distinguish the two. In that case, I would move the light farther away from the background or change the bulb to a lower wattage.

Do not use a rheostat to decrease the power to any photographic lamp—this will drastically shift the color balance toward red. A photolamp's color temperature is guaranteed only at rated wattage output.

After everything is adjusted to your satisfaction, turn on both lights for your final meter reading, using the designated method for your type of handheld meter. This measurement will serve as the basis for your film test.

Using Built-in Light Meters
Seeing What's Right in Front of You

It's very difficult to measure lighting ratios with built-in meters and even more difficult for beginners to interpret. However, you can get a rough idea of the relative strength of the background light to the main light once you have the camera position established and locked into place on the tripod. With only the main light on, meter as you normally would, with all the precautions mentioned in chapter 1 about light meters. Mark the position of the art object carefully, and then take it out of the set. After turning off the main light, turn on the backlight and make a measurement. Apply the same adjustments mentioned in the last section.

Background Variations
In Four-Part Harmony

If you replace the mottled backdrop with a white wall, a background meter reading of equal value or up to one stop higher than the main light would produce a clean white to a bright white background on the film. Photographers call this poster lighting. The object appears to pick up a glow from the light hitting and reflecting off all the edges.

Increasing the lighting ratio and making the background even brighter generates the risk of creating a substantial amount of lens flare, thus creating ghostlike photo images. In this instance, the background light would simply overwhelm the main light and bounce uncontrollably all around your lens rather than proceeding straight through the lens like it should. Very light backgrounds are possible, but several tests may be needed. During your film test, make a series of progressively lighter background exposures and carefully note the light position and power settings. When the film comes back, find the setting where the flare first appears, then adjust the background lights down at least a one-half f-stop; one full stop down would be even safer.

Handheld meter users should take the reading from the main light only for their exposure settings. Built-in meter users should take their final reading with both lights on and open up one-half to one full stop to compensate for the strong backlighting in this situation.

You can choose to photographically turn the white wall different shades of gray by reducing the light falling on the background two to four stops below that of the main light. You may have to move the art piece a considerable distance from the wall to allow for enough fall-off to accomplish the more radical background transformation to a dark gray.

Environmental Factors
Eliminating Film Pollution

Every time we set up lights for photography, some light gets bounced around the walls, floor, and ceiling. Inevitably, some of this scattered light affects the color balance in your photographs; for example, if there are pale green walls and green carpeting around the shooting area, expect to see a greenish tinge in the lighter areas in the photograph. In this case, shoot as many film tests as needed to find the right filtration to correct the color imbalance (see page 226).

Within the same hypothetical setup, white backgrounds are most prone to pick up color influences from the room. A professional photo studio is typically composed of a combination of white, black, or gray to minimize unwanted color effects; if you don't have such a "neutral" shooting area, try building your set in the middle of the room. If you must be close to a wall with strong color, cover it with a white or black paper backdrop, or improvise with a white sheet. If you must put your set on (or near) a floor with strong color, use a wider backdrop or cover the adjacent areas with a neutral color drop cloth. I save all of my used backdrop paper precisely for these situations, using it to cover as much of the wall or floor as necessary.

You can use this same principle to add color to the object. For example, a bright blue backdrop will reflect blue light around the set, off reflectors and into the object, for better or worse. If you are shooting nonglossy white vases with this blue background, all the edges are going to have an obvious blue cast. However, with a black matte vase on the same blue backdrop, this cast may not be noticeable or objectionable—indeed the blue reflections may add to the overall effect.

Light reflecting off the art object itself may create unwanted color shifts in localized areas of the backdrop. Recently, I photographed a light green object that I had to shoot on a glossy, white surface. Not only was the hard reflection of the object green, but everything except the brightest highlights was also green. This type of color shift is corrected by adding the necessary filtration (see page 226).

One more possible source of color contamination to watch out for is from the reflector materials used in your set. As mattes and foam boards age and yellow, so do the photographic results. This may not be bad if your film tends to produce results on the bluish side, but replacing aging reflectors is gen-

Figure 4.14A. Mixed media (ceramic and rice paper) by Stanley Edwards, 5"w, 1991. Matte objects such as this cannot reflect the dark lines created by the spokes of a photo umbrella. The spokes would be readily apparent on objects that have broad, shiny surfaces like those in figure 4.5.

erally cheaper and less time consuming than doing a number of film tests to correct for the color shift.

Lighting Option 2
The Great Umbrella Cover-up

Everyone expects to see photographic umbrellas when walking into any photo studio. These umbrellas open and close just like the rainy-day type for quick breakdown and storage. They come in a variety of sizes and use eight to twelve spokes to sup-

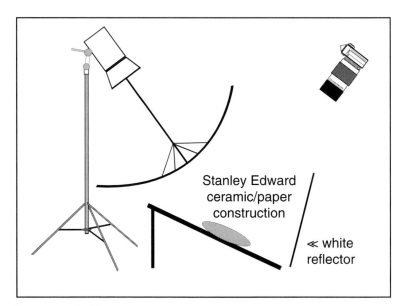

Stanley Edward
ceramic/paper
construction

≪ white
reflector

Figure 4.14B. Side view of setup for figure 4.14A.

Figure 4.15. Same as figure
4.14A, but photographed on
black velvet. Some grant applications require either black or
white backgrounds in all photos.

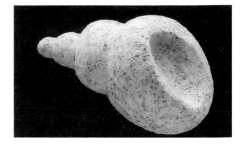

port the material when open.

The problem is that these spokes have a way of showing up
(either as bright reflections or dark lines) in the broad, flat
glossy, or semigloss smoothly curved areas of the artwork. The
bright octagonal reflections are not very appealing.

If all the work you do is matte, an umbrella matched to your
needs will work well for lighting in most situations. Used in
pairs or sets of four, they should be all that is needed to take
photos of three-dimensional and flat artwork.

Strobe heads and the better tungsten light heads have a slot
and locking wing nut to secure and correctly position any
umbrella. Accessory clamps are available for the lights that
don't and will allow you to attach the umbrella to a stand or any
other support.

Umbrellas can be divided into two categories: shoot-through
and bounce. A few manufacturers make umbrellas that convert
from one type to another, but these are nearly as expensive as
two separate umbrellas and offer no real advantage. Choosing
the type to buy is a matter of knowing which one does a better
job for your specific project.

Shoot-Through Umbrellas

Shoot-through umbrellas are made of a white translucent
material that softens and diffuses the light that passes through
the umbrella on its way to the set/object. It also spreads the
light across a much wider angle. Both of these factors contrib-
ute to a loss in light intensity from one-half to one full stop
when compared with direct lighting.

Figure 4.16A. Paper sculpture by Richard Tuttle, 1989. The umbrella is positioned as closely to the wall as possible since both it and much of the artwork is white. The positioning created a dark sharp line around the bottom edge of the piece to separate it from the wall. At the top edge of the art, this lighting emphasized the textural difference between the art and wall.

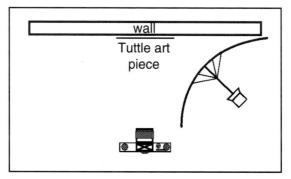

Figure 4.16B. This illustration shows a top view of the lighting setup for figure 4.16A.

A portion of the light is also reflected backward off the umbrella and will scatter around the room (see figure 3.12, page 47). This may or may not produce a desirable effect, depending on the color of the walls and floor. If the color is fairly neutral, this scattered light adds a little overall illumination and partially fills in the shadows areas. If strong, objectionable colors exist throughout the environment, the preventative measures mentioned in the previous section will help minimize the room effects.

Shoot-through umbrellas can be placed very close to the art object, as long as the umbrella itself doesn't show up in the frame area. The closer distance allows the use of smaller f-stops as well as enlarging the apparent size of the light source, providing the desired large "natural" light.

Figure 4.14 is a photo of a construction by Stanley Edwards that is meant to be hung on a wall. However, it doesn't need to be photographed that way. I used a setup for flat artwork similar to the one in figure 3.6 (chapter 3, page 38) but with only one light. I positioned the one umbrella high and slightly to the right of the object to place the shadow down and to it's left. A silver reflector, placed opposite the light and just outside the frame area, was added to fill in the shadow.

I later rephotographed this piece with almost exactly the same setup, but I used a black background (figure 4.15) to meet the requirements for a grant application. This allowed the judges to use multiple projectors and view several slides at once without the intrusive borders of the frame. Losing the shadow makes the artwork look as if it's floating in space.

To photograph a paper construction by Richard Tuttle (figure 4.16), the umbrella was positioned slightly above the piece and close to the wall on which it was mounted. Since this piece has

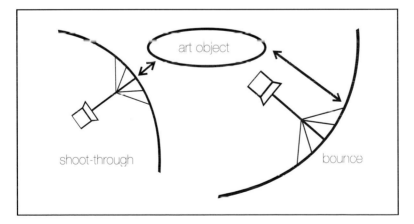

Figure 4.17. The construction of a shoot-through umbrella allows it to be positioned closer to an object than a bounce umbrella. The bounce umbrella would need to be larger in diameter to create a similar lighting effect as a smaller shoot-through.

Figure 4.18. Limited-edition porcelain for Artes Magnus by George Segal. "Classical Still Life," 1990, 13½"h 3 201½"w 3 12"d. The extremely matte surface of this sculpture necessitated a more directional lighting. The silver-lined umbrella used for this shot scatters the light considerably less than do shoot-through umbrellas, creating brighter highlights and sharper shadows.

little depth, the light skimming across the surface enhances the texture and its three-dimensionality. The exaggerated shadows were not filled in to add to this effect.

Bounce Umbrellas

Bounce umbrellas are similar in construction to the shoot-through type except that they have an opaque outer surface that stops any light from passing through. This produces an indirect light that is reflected, or "bounced," so the tip of the umbrella should be aimed away from the object and set in order to illuminate it. The bounce umbrella can't be placed as close to the object as the shoot-through type and has to be larger to produce the same broad "natural" light (see figure 4.17).

The efficiency of this arrangement is determined by the material used to "bounce" the light. A matte white fabric will produce a more diffuse light than a silver mylar. Because it is more reflective, the silver mylar loses less light in the bounce and af-fords a smaller f-stop, though it does produce harsher shadows. For some matte, monochrome artwork, such as figure 4.18, harsher lighting is exactly what is needed. I used a 54-inch silver umbrella above and just behind this sculpture, and no fill card, to keep all the contrast I could. Note how the

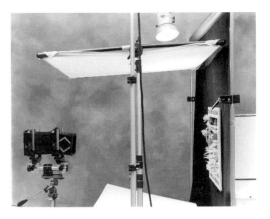

Figure 4.19. Side view of set for Lori Casella's "New York Flower Show." Mixed media, 14" x 14", 1991. Note how the light is placed in close proximity to the diffuson material to create noticeable shadows seen in figure 4.20. Moving the light farther away from the diffusion material would scatter the light over a larger area and create softer shadows and more shadow detail.

background rapidly fades to black, producing something close to a spotlight effect.

Some manufacturers make a silver reflector that can also be covered with a white matte liner, allowing you to switch whenever necessary. (Also available, but not really applicable here, are gold-lined umbrellas that are used to warm up flesh tones in portrait and fashion photography.)

Lighting Option 3
Make or Buy Your Own

Although ceilings can make great "natural" light sources, they don't offer the necessary range of control. Being able to move

Figure 4.20. Final photograph—produced using the lighting setup shown in figure 4.19.

and adjust our natural-looking light allows us greater flexibility and adaptability in achieving an acceptable lighting solution. The focus of the next lighting option is really simple: we shoot light through a diffusion material as large as necessary to achieve a "natural" look.

Figure 4.19 shows the set I used to photograph one of Lori Casella's art projects for her final portfolio at New York's School of Visual Arts (where graduating seniors turn in photos only of their projects for grading). I shot light through a translucent white fabric that was wrapped around a frame (42-inches square) made from PVC tubing.

I kept the light head close to the fabric to create a more directional, "high noon" feeling in the photograph (figure 4.20) to match the theme of the subject matter. A softer, less directional light would have been created if the light head had been farther away. Only one reflector directly beneath the set was needed to decrease the shadow intensity to an acceptable level for four-color reproduction. Even though I was hired to shoot only presentation transparencies, which allow a much wider lighting range, it is my practice to shoot everything to publication standards, should the artist require it for later use.

Store-Bought Lighting

There are several manufacturers who make frames in a variety of sizes, as well as several choices of diffusion or reflective materials. A frame I bought is hinged at each corner and has two break joints to fold it for storage. The diffusion material is form-fitted (like sheets) and is held taut by strong elastic angled across each corner. With a total weight of two pounds, the frame is light enough to be held at extreme angles by inexpensive clamps on lightweight stands. The frame and diffuser cost about $75, and a couple clamps cost $25 more. I use this lighting package for most of my demonstrations, since it can be set up quickly and is easy to transport. The frame is durable enough to withstand heavy use—a lifetime investment for the occasional user.

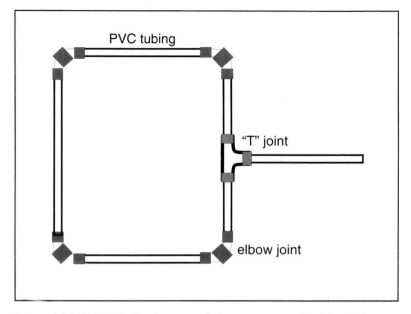

Figure 4.21. PVC diffusion frame made from common plumbing tubing.

Homemade Frames
Curing the Expensive Equipment Headache

PVC. For those on a budget or anyone wishing to avoid the expense, you can easily make a diffusion frame and buy suitable diffusion material for a fraction of the price. It may not break down so easily, if at all. But this shouldn't be a problem if you never foresee leaving your studio with it.

PVC tubing is cheap and available at many discount stores. Four elbow joints, four pieces of tubing, and some PVC glue are all you need to complete your frame.

If you put in a T-joint in the middle of one of the sides (figure 4.21) you can fashion your own brackets or add an extension arm that will allow you to easily rotate the frame on one axis. This material's rigidity makes it possible to hold the frame securely from one side with little flexing.

Wood. It's just as easy to make a frame out of wood. Plan your rectangle or square by using simple butt joints held together by L brackets and wood screws at each corner. Select wood 1-inch square or smaller in order to keep the frame as lightweight and thin as possible. This will also help keep overall costs to a minimum.

Expect a lot of flex with this type of frame. It will need to be supported or suspended at each corner. Judging from my own personal experience, I find that suspension is the easier choice. Screw an eye hook into the back of the frame near each corner and put four eye hooks in a similar but slightly enlarged configuration in the ceiling directly above your shooting area. A cord, rope, or filament from each corner to the ceiling will allow you to suspend the frame at any angle by simply adjusting the length of the line.

The beauty of this arrangement is that it allows unrestricted access to the set from all sides, which simplifies placing and adjusting any object or reflector on the set. It also provides an extra margin of safety since the frame can easily be held in place by the other lines if one line should slip or break.

Lights can be positioned above the frame on stands next to the set. The closer the light source is to the frame, the more directional the light and the heavier the shadows: the farther away the light source, the more diffuse the light is, and the less distinct the shadows.

My favorite home-built frame was a 9 × 9-foot one that I made from 1-inch-square wood. I shopped around until I found a cheap white curtain material that was the right translucency. I stretched this tautly from side to side and secured it using a staple gun. The eye hooks in the ceiling were very widely spaced to allow maximum vertical and horizontal adjustment. Quick-release attachments (climbing carabiniers) held a long filament rope to each corner of the frame. The rope was fed through the hook on the ceiling and then tied to a side wall using a cleat arrangement like that found on boats. I

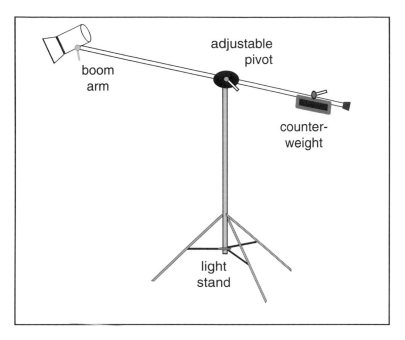

Figure 4.22. A boom arm.

often hung this frame vertically (or nearly so) and cut a small camera hole for such occasions. When not in use, the camera hole was replaced with a patch of similar material held in place by four small Velcro patches. Total cost for this very large fixture was $50, with $20 of that going for the expensive nylon rope.

Booms and Stands
A New Balancing Act

A boom arm (see figure 4.22) attached to a wall or a light stand is needed to center the light source over the diffusion frame, producing direct axis lighting (the shadows come straight at the camera). There are many varieties and sizes available on the market; most of the freestanding ones have a

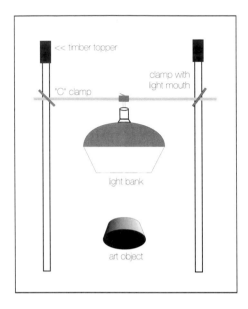

Figure 4.23. A homemade support used to suspend a large light over the setup.

movable counterbalance to prevent the equipment from falling over. Make all adjustments of the counterweight far enough away from the set to avoid catastrophe. Double-check the security of the weight and light source after every adjustment.

Several lights can be attached to one boom arm with additional clamps. Make sure that they hold the lights securely and that they are properly tightened. Be aware that if the additional lights are widely spaced, subtle and conflicting shadows will appear; try to aim them so that they overlap to preserve the "one light" illusion.

As an alternative, it's relatively simple to fashion a boom out of lumber or metal and attach it to the wall or ceiling. You can use cut-to-height 2 × 3-inch wood with spring-loaded tops as uprights with a cross pole secured by C-clamps (see figure 4.23). Build your photo set under the cross pole and attach as many lights as you need with the appropriate clamps. This homemade boom will be about one-third the cost of the store-bought boom and is equally adjustable. All you'll lose is perhaps a bit of speed and convenience. Most big photo studios have

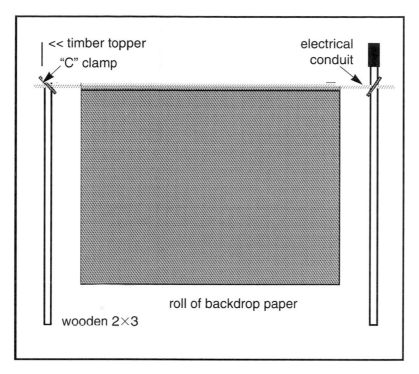

Figure 4.24. A background paper support using the same materials as seen in figure 4.23. A single 2 x 3 beam and timber topper can support clamp lights or large foam-core reflectors.

several sets of these spring-loaded uprights. However, since the lumber is cut to size for the ceiling height, they will not easily adapt to other locations.

These same uprights also make excellent backdrop paper holders. Use a piece of electrical conduit or a tubular closet rod long enough to stick through the roll of paper, leaving a foot on each side. For a 9-foot-wide backdrop, the conduit, or pole, should be at least 11 feet long. Lay the paper on the floor and position the uprights about 3 inches outside the end of the roll. Put a C-clamp at the same height on each pole (see figure 4.24). Pick the paper up from one end, holding the rod or conduit so that it doesn't slide out, and slip the other end into the distant

C-clamp. Then place the side you are holding into its clamp by first moving the rod into the roll and then pulling it out through the clamp, leaving about a 6-inch overhang.

Manufactured backdrop stands are usually made out of aluminum and are easily adjusted to fit a wide range of ceiling heights. Expect to pay $100 to $300 for either arrangement.

Diffusion Materials
Organizing Your Scattered Light

Fabric is the most readily available diffusion material to use with your light frames. Translucent white curtain material is both cheap and durable. Sailcloth is another option, though a bit more expensive. Whatever the fabric, try to choose a pure white, with no distinct pattern other than its natural weave. Any pattern has a tendency to show up in the reflections of the light source, especially on a broad, glossy area. So will pronounced wrinkles. If the art object is especially flat and glossy, even small ripples will show up and ruin otherwise perfect photos.

Choose a fabric that offers a good compromise between diffusion and transmission. A fabric that creates too much light diffusion will result in a lot of lost lighting power. There is a point where the diffusion effects cease to change but the transmission of light continues to drop. If the fabric creates too little light diffusion, shadows will be more sharply defined and the light quality will appear harsh. To test for the right balance, look through the fabric and see if shapes can be distinguished as light and dark areas, but without detail.

Most fabrics eventually yellow with age, but this can easily be remedied with a little bleach. Some of the synthetic materials are pretty indestructible so long as you don't place the lights right on top of them. All photo lights produce lots of heat that can scorch or burn even the most resistant materials.

Plastic shower curtains, another source of cheap diffusion, are favorites of TV and small film production crews and are available in both clear frosted and white frosted. Even more care must be used with these since it only takes a little heat to make the plastic melt.

Also available at most art supply stores is architectural tracing paper (vellum), which comes in rolls of various widths and lengths. This paper can easily be taped to the PVC or stapled to wood frames and is cheap enough to throw away and replace when it "ages" too much on the frame. Tracing vellum is great as a diffusion material for many photo purposes, so I always have a roll handy. A roll can last for years.

Specialty plastic stores (and a few art stores) often have rolls of thin diffusion materials under a number of brand names. They are twice as expensive as tracing vellum, but many are also more durable, and can be cleaned with strong solvents as they age or get soiled. In large metropolitan areas, shops that cater to photographers and set-builders have a vast assortment of these materials on hand and their sales staff has the expertise to help you make a good choice.

Plexiglas is an excellent diffuser but is extremely heavy when compared to the other materials mentioned. To use it as an overhead light source would demand heavier stands, clamps, and fixtures and therefore more cash outlay, and it wouldn't necessarily produce better photographic results. It could, however, be placed vertically and used as an excellent sidelight with little extra equipment (chapter 5, page 94).

Lighting Option 4
Running All the Way to the Bank

By combining both the bounce umbrella and the diffusion light frame, we get a piece of equipment called a *light bank.* Lightweight, portable, and expensive ($200–$1,000), these banks don't allow any stray light to bounce around the room and are therefore most efficient. A wall-mounted boom arm ($125) or a freestanding counterbalanced heavy-duty boom ($250–$400) is needed to position and control the bank. This is the equipment I use both in the studio and on location to make my work easy, but it does come at a high cost that can only be justified by high usage. If you can afford it without sapping money from other important areas in your work, give it a try by renting it from a professional shop before purchasing your own.

At some point in his or her career, every still-life photographer has built a light bank out of necessity. Up until a few years ago, foam core was the favored material on the East coast, with wood construction being the king of the West. Photographers designed most of these homemade banks after studying several manufactured ones and then tailoring them for their specific needs.

The portable light banks are the rage today because fewer and fewer photographers have their own studios, renting space only when needed. Several artists could purchase and share a light bank because it is completely mobile.

Shooting Your First Test Shot
In Self-Defense

Unless you are prepared to waste a lot of film, time, and money, it's important to shoot a film test on one subject to see how everything is working or not working. I can't guarantee that you will progress smoothly and produce perfect shots the first time. That's generally not the case, even if you've been doing this for fifteen years, like I have. If you follow my advice and checklists, you will come close on the first try, and do much better than you ever have done on your own. This section assumes that you already have chosen, bought, or made your lighting.

I like to build the set and lighting to accommodate the largest art piece I need to shoot in each session. Smaller objects will always fit on larger sets; the reverse may not be true and may lead to additional and unnecessary work in rebuilding the set.

The film test is needed to establish the correct exposure and filtration for professional results. Once that is achieved, *you can shoot any other object down to half the size on the same set and be able to predict and control the end results.* Just place another object in your setup and shoot. It's as easy as that.

The only things you *always* need to adjust are the reflectors and fill lights to show off each object to the best advantage, unless the shape and texture of the objects is identical. And if you do change the main light, you now have a baseline from which to make the necessary comparisons and adjustments.

At this point in the process, refer back to the sections "Keeping Track of Your Efforts," "Final Checks and Common Errors," "The All-Important Exposure Bracket," and "Detail Shots," pages 45–52. Just ignore the remarks about looking for unwanted glare on oil paintings.

Final Checklist for Shooting Three-Dimensional Art

Use the following checklist before shooting each new piece of artwork.

1. Arrange and completely secure the lighting, taping all cords down or out of the way.
2. Make sure the work area is free of adverse or external light.
3. Check for proper setting of film speed on light meter.
4. Set the aperture and f-stop for the correct exposure solution.
5. Check the image in the viewfinder for composition, and for reflectors showing in the frame area.
6. Focus critically and inspect art objects for unwanted glare and/or reflections.
7. Check that all controls are on tight on tripod head, legs, and camera attachment.
8. Check for unwanted glare on the lens.
9. Make sure film is properly loaded and advancing.
10. Eliminate as much vibration as possible.
11. Make one-half–f-stop–exposure brackets.
12. Check viewfinder to see if the image has moved.
13. Set up the next object and repeat.

5

Special Three-Dimensional Problems

Special Cures, Exceptional Solutions

Side Lighting

Top lighting, as described in chapter 4, is a wonderful lighting method for most three-dimensional artwork, but it won't work for everything. One example is Shauna Vineberg's construction (figure 5.1). If top lighting were used, shadows from the top frame would fall on the figures below, and the shadows from the figures would fall on the bed. I did set this up at first with top light, thinking that a slightly more exaggerated back lighting (light coming from a 20 to 30 degree angle) would create the desired effect. Although it would have produced results that were perfectly adequate, I knew that the image could be lighted to produce a more dramatic result.

In the final arrangement (figure 5.2), I placed the light source (the black box on the stand) at almost a right angle to the lens/object axis, but just in front on the object to throw the shadows slightly away from the camera. The extreme angle of this light enhanced the texture of the figures and door since it literally skimmed along the surface. This is an extreme example of what is called *modeling* light or light specifically used to enhance or define the outer structure of the subject.

The sidelight is also placed very close to the set to create the bright highlight on the edges of the floating figures closest to the light. The far end of the figure is about one-third of the total

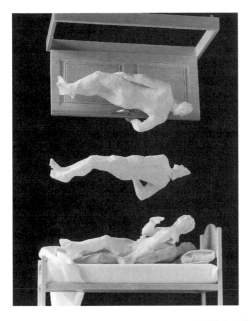

Figure 5.1. Mixed media by Shauna Vineberg, "Dreams," 1991. Strong side lighting added drama to this photograph and also brought out the surface texture and dimension of the white objects. The threads suspending the figures were easily retouched out on the black-and-white print. Figure 5.3 shows the photo before retouching.

Figure 5.2. View from behind the camera used in figure 5.1.

Figure 5.3. This unre-
touched photo shows the
threads used to suspend
the object. Retouching
them out contributes to the
photograph's illusion.

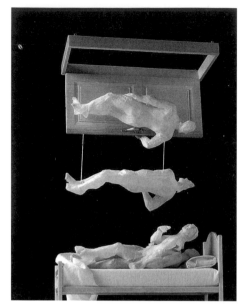

distance farther away, so the light at that end is nearly one full stop down in intensity, creating contrast (more light and more dark) in an otherwise very low contrast object. In this setup (figure 5.2) the farther away I pulled the light source, the lower the contrast was.

The black background was chosen to add to the contrast illusion. It also makes retouching the lines of fishing filament as simple as possible, in both the black-and-white print and the 4 × 5 transparency (see figure 5.3). A special photographic dye, used for spotting black-and-white prints, was applied with a 000 camel hair brush in several diluted applications until the white lines were completely blended in. Read the dye's instructions carefully and make several practice runs on reject prints before working on your final print. It's also a good idea to make extra copies of any print you intend to retouch, in case your first retouch effort is less than stellar.

This print dye worked equally well on the emulsion side (the slightly duller and textured side that the light strikes) of the

4 × 5 transparency because there was no color involved. Since we view transparencies from the reverse side of the emulsion, and the area around the lines was maximum black, even a very poor retouch job would go unnoticed as long as the lines were heavily filled in.

Retouching colors into or out of transparencies is a very tricky job best left to experts who have several years' experience. It is often necessary to bleach one color out before adding or creating another color. This must be done with great precision under heavy optical magnification since the image is relatively small at 4 × 5 inches. It is nearly impossible to retouch 35mm slides. Larger professional labs offer retouching services at $50 per hour or higher. Ask for an estimate in writing before the retouching work starts. Some seemingly simple tasks may be quite labor intensive and therefore costly.

The light source I used for figure 5.3 is a specialized electronic flash head called a *box light*. Although diffused, the light coming from these boxes tends to be more directional, producing deeper shadows than larger light banks. It is also considerably more efficient, generating more lighting power per watt, because the light is not spread over such a large area. It is most useful for smaller objects, like the one in figure 5.2, or for placing a small highlight on a larger object. I often place small objects, such as jewelry, directly onto my box lights, using them as both a surface and a source of underlighting (covered later in this chapter).

The box light's construction is similar to light boxes we view slides on, only it is made a bit deeper to guarantee perfect evenness of the light. You can see the back of mine and its mounting bracket. Inside the box are several electronic flashtubes, whose light exits through a 12 × 15-inch white plexi sheet on the far side. You can build your own box light out of wood and several photo lamps to provide illumination. Drill equally spaced holes in the back panel for a tight fit for the light sockets if you intend to use screw-in photo flood lamps of 250–500 watts. Be sure that the sockets used can handle that amount of power. If you want to use quartz lamps, their sockets can just be screwed onto the inside surface of the back panel. The inside should be painted white or silver. The silver paint increases the efficiency at the expense of lower diffusion.

A 12 × 15-inch light will need four lamps; larger ones will need even more. The idea of the design is to overwhelm the interior of the box with light. This will generate considerable heat. Drill several additional holes on each side of the box (except the front) for ventilation. If these cause unwanted light to fall on your set, simply cover the offending vents with heavy tape. If the box still gets too hot, install a small exhaust fan on the rear panel of the unit. This will help extend bulb life considerably.

Wire the lamps so that you can turn each on or off individually. This will allow you to conserve power or keep the temperatures down whenever maximum power is not needed. It also allows you to modulate the light from side to side and corner to corner, creating different lighting effects.

Platters and Plates

Decorative plates should be shot essentially the way they are usually displayed—held vertically on a stand (figure 5.4). The natural lighting setup is the same one described in chapter 4, the only difference is that the plate is placed a little farther back in the set to make it ever so slightly lit from the front.

Figure 5.5 shows the side view of the lighting arrangement used in this shot. The platter itself has very little depth, front to back. *Note that the shallower the depth, the closer to perpendicular (90 degrees) the light must be in relation to the camera axis.* The platter, in this instance, was pushed toward the back of the set (the light source was kept in position) until there was a clearly defined highlight on the indentation (figure 5.6). This also produced a nice white highlight around the rim at the top.

The light source was nearly at right angles to the plane of the plate, enhancing the texture of the metalwork by creating

Figure 5.4. A seventeenth-century metal plate by Adolph Gap, approximately 24"w. There is very little depth to this object when photographed from this angle. The lighting needs to be almost 90 degrees off the lens axis to create the highlight area shown in figure 5.6.

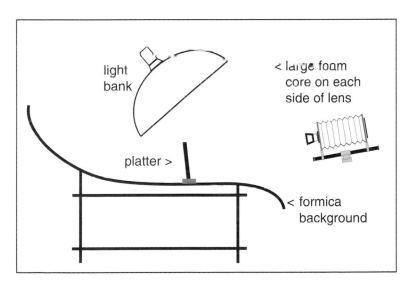

Figure 5.5. Side-view diagram of the lighting setup for figure 5.4.

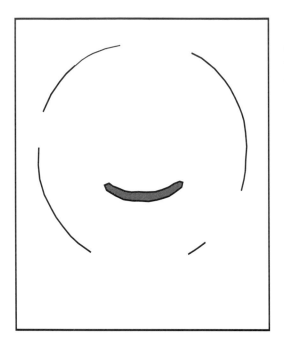

Figure 5.6. The high-light area as illus-trated gives the viewer a visual clue about the relative depth of this platter.

highlights at the top of each protrusion. At this point in the process, the front of the platter had a lot of bright small high-lights but was black everywhere else.

Being highly reflective, the platter was acting like a large mir-ror in a darkened room. I had to use large pieces of white foam board positioned on both sides of the camera to create reflec-tions onto the mirrorlike surface of the platter. The closer I positioned the foam board, the brighter the reflections; the far-ther away, the dimmer the reflections but the larger the board had to be to create the "seamless" look. (See figure 5.6.)

Hiding the Stand

The ceramic work entitled "Jacob Wrestling with the Angel" (figure 5.7) is very glossy and nearly flat. The only photographic clue that there is some depth to the work is the highlight at the bottom of the plate. The setup and execution was exactly the same as for Adolph Gap's piece (see figures 5.4 and 5.5), except

Figure 5.7. This plate appears to have very little depth. The reflector just to the side of the camera produced a very subtle highlight around the plate's edge.

Figure 5.8. Side view of figure 5.7. A heavy support is often needed to hold objects up at extreme angles. Use as much adhesive as possible to ensure that the object will remain in position.

that no stand was used. A side view of the set (figure 5.8) reveals how this illusion is accomplished.

The heavily weighted quart-size jar seen in figure 5.8 provides the necessary stability upon which to lean so expensive an art piece. Jeweler's wax holds the plate to the jar at the top, and a piece of Fun-Tack on the bottom holds the plate in position on the formica surface. Before shooting, I carefully checked that the blob of Fun-Tack adhesive on the surface was not visible from the camera angle. This is easy to overlook, so do check it to be sure none of the tacking will show in the photograph.

If you must leave an object set up like this for any length of time and you are not in the act of shooting, place something equally as heavy and immovable in front of the object to prevent it from tipping over. Don't tempt the fates by placing complete faith in the adhesives. Disaster waits for those who do. I prefer to keep my perfect record of never damaging any work of art.

Figure 5.9. Light skims across this platter's surface, much as in figure 5.4. In this instance, the photographic setup was configured to shoot the object vertically rather than horizontally.

Variations

The platter in figure 5.9 is quite tall and heavy and was meant to be hung on a wall. I shot this photo at a museum, where it was not possible to hang the piece. The art handler placed the art on tabletop raised 12 inches off the floor with the camera positioned directly above (see figure 5.10). I stretched the 36-inch-wide roll of tracing vellum (see diffusion materials, pages 89–90) between two light stands. The light head, positioned behind the vellum, was adjusted vertically and horizontally to create the right amount of texture and highlight.

I hung a large white reflector directly beneath the lens to add enough fill light to raise light levels in the shadow areas and ensure good offset printing press reproduction quality. I placed white reflectors along the sides to create the highlights around the edge of the plate and separate it from the black velour background.

Except for the white reflectors on the surface, this setup is showing exactly the same lighting principle as the setup used in the Adolph Gap photo (figures 5.4 and 5.5). There, the camera axis was horizontal; here the camera axis is vertical.

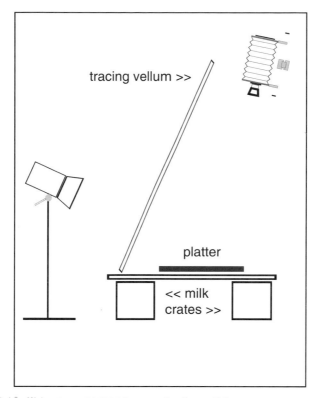

Figure 5.10. Side view of lighting setup for figure 5.9.

Service Sets

While we're talking about plates, let me illustrate a couple of different ways to handle sets of plates. The first example (figure 5.11) shows a complete serving set designed by Patrick Loughran. The background was a 4 × 8-foot gray formica sweep and the lighting was set up in the same way as in figure 5.4. The two plates are supported by small metal stands (hence the two small hooks at the bottom), but overlap quite a bit.

If nothing in this photo overlapped but was spread out horizontally, the resulting composition would be a long row of ceramics with a lot of open area at the top and bottom. The

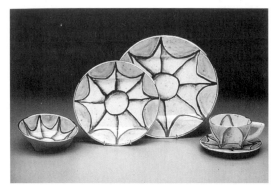

Figure 5.11. Ceramic service set, Patrick Loughran, 1988. Although this photograph is an accurate representation of this artist's work, graphically it is too long and narrow. This not only makes the objects appear small, it also makes the composition boring. See figure 5.12 for a different interpretation.

camera would also have to be pulled farther back to accommodate the increased width, making the ceramics reproduce even smaller on film. This type of composition is visually uninteresting and diminishes your work in more ways than one.

Since the same pattern repeats itself on each ceramic piece, I really don't have to show every piece in its entirety to show the design. It is most important to indicate the relationship in size among the plates, which is easily achieved by placing them close together. I placed the camera at an angle high enough to allow the viewer to see inside the cup and bowl, where the pattern repeated. At any higher camera angles, the round plates would begin to look more like ovals, something I wanted to avoid. To prevent this from happening, while still allowing the viewer to see clearly into the bowl, I had to cheat a bit. I accomplished this by propping up the bowl's base at the back, slightly tipping the bowl toward the lens.

There are more ways than one to effectively photograph this set (figure 5.12). I chose a 45-degree camera angle so that the viewer could clearly see both the sides and the insides of the cup and bowl. As with figure 5.11, since the pattern is clearly established on one of the pieces, I could let the edges of the plates bleed right out of the frame and still indicate the design. I was able move in even closer to the ceramic set in figure 5.12, allowing for an even larger reproduction on film, giving the photo even more impact.

I kept the light very low to emphasize and bring out the

Figure 5.12. This version fills the frame better and reproduces the objects larger. The space in the upper left corner allows enough area to imprint the artist's name.

ridges on plates. One well-positioned foam board (at the front, left) was all that was needed to produce the necessary fill light. I aimed the main light source at the white formica just behind the serving set. This negative white space balances nicely with the denser feeling of the plates at the bottom of the frame, giving the photo a natural gravity.

The top white area also leaves enough space to drop in the artist's or gallery's name, an important consideration if you know the photo will be used as a display ad or direct-mail piece where this print information must be included. Including the information in this way allows for larger images of your artwork than would be possible if this information had its own separate space. However, this requires a bit more planning and prior knowledge of the size and shape of the type to be included. The end result can be a much more visually effective and interesting photo and definitely worth the effort.

Even More Plates

I had a challenging assignment to make an interesting photo of plate sets that were designed on commission by Neil Flavin, best known for his neon work. The top of his plates and bowls were shiny porcelain white. The bottoms were produced in various shocking neon colors that were meant to be seen mostly as reflections on the plate below. This creative concept was very tough to photograph.

After experimenting around with the layout (six different

Figure 5.13. Limited-edition porcelain for Artes Magnus by Dan Flavin. Service diner, "For André Raynaud," 1991. This photo is by far more interpretive than previous examples, but fits nicely with the artist's idea for this commissioned work. The artist is well known for his neon work. The diffusion filter creates a similar mood in this photo.

colors, four sets of one plate and one bowl) for a couple days, I came up with the design shown in figure 5.13. Trying to add something extra, I put the whole composition on a white plexi light table (figure 5.14). A light table illuminates objects from underneath, making them appear as if they are floating in space, while it floods the entire area with light (read the glassware section later in this chapter for more about light tables). One light was positioned to throw raw, direct light into the creases between the plates to bounce around the color of their backs. This undiffused light also provided the illumination for the inside of each bowl. I spent at least two hours moving this light around and observing the effects. The difference between a good photo and a great photo can be a matter of millimeters.

Observe how this raw light produces sharp, dark shadows and just a tiny white highlight on the lip of each plate. The reflector is only 7 inches wide, so it produces the understandably small reflection of a 7-inch light source at a distance of about 3 feet from the object. Using this narrow light source is the antithesis of everything I have told you so far—but here it works.

Every time I try something different, it's hard not to keep going. For this photo I turned off the bottom lights altogether, leaving hard, nasty shadows that were softened by using a diffusion filter *on the lens.* Diffusion is diffusion, no matter where you get it from. These filters on the lens soften both contrast and sharpness, according to the amount of diffusion designed into the filter. The softness in the photo mirrors the soft light effect of most neon lamps on white walls.

Tilting the camera was almost an afterthought. It helped break up the rigid pattern effect and added some movement. This composition also opened up enough negative space for a logo or other typography in the upper right corner. This interpretive photo is much closer to advertising than documentation, but that was the assignment. There may be times when you need to photograph your

Figure 5.14. Setup for figure 5.3, showing the porcelain on a light table. The light underneath was turned off for this final version.

work with more of an eye on artistic composition than on pure presentation.

In these instances, the additional effort will help get more attention for your ad or mailing piece since you are most often competing with many other images. It will also help get your work published. It may be counterproductive to shoot all your work this way since doing so focuses as much attention and criticism on your marketing skills as it does on your art.

Large Bowls, Jugs

Wayne Higby's bowl (figure 5.15) was a delight to visually explore and photograph. Wayne spent as much time working on the inside of the bowl as on the outside. I chose the camera angle I used to include just enough of the interior to explicate the idea of the total design. When I began with a standard light-

Figure 5.15. Ceramic bowl by Wayne Higby, 1990. The reflector card inside the bowl adds both illumination and highlight to the interior that is visible to the camera.

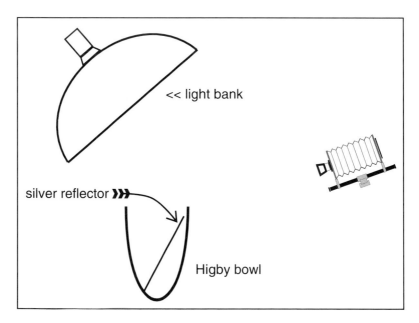

Figure 5.16. Side-view diagram of the setup for figure 5.15.

Figure 5.17. Early American water vessel. One silver reflector card creates a subtle highlight, breaking up an otherwise large, undistinguished flat outside area. The other card, inside the vessel, creates a highlight inside that appears to be coming from the same light source that created the outside highlight.

ing configuration, the *inside* of the bowl appeared too dark and textureless.

I easily remedied this by carefully placing additional reflector cards inside the bowl—but out of sight from the camera (diagram 5.16). A white card on the left and a silver card on the right were cut to size and used to create the reflections and texture.

Another example of this technique is the photo (figure 5.17) of an early American stoneware piece. The inside was a very dark brown and looked totally featureless. Placing one silver reflector inside the vessel made all the difference, and helped restore the illusion of volume and curve. A large silver reflector used to create the highlight on the outside (see lighting diagram, figure 5.18) helped bring out the surface texture. Both this card and the inside card were on the same side of the piece and at the same angle to keep the reflections consistent.

Extremely Shiny

It only took one look at this shiny black teapot (figure 5.19) for me to know that getting a good shot of it was going to take some work. First, I tried placing it on a light table, which some-

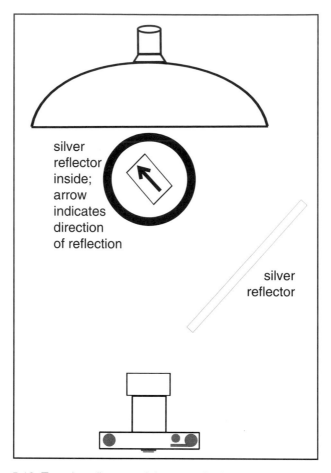

Figure 5.18. Top-view diagram of the setup for figure 5.17.

times works with objects like this, but the rounded nature of this piece created conflicting sets of bright highlights. So I went back to the drawing board.

The real challenge when shooting any highly reflective object is to create pleasing reflections on the object itself. Realize that everything around the object will be *sharply* mirrored off the object. This includes the light source, the background, the fill cards, the overhead sprinkler system—everything in direct line-

Figure 5.19. Mass-produced glazed ceramic from Japan, c. 1935. Creating pleasantly shaped high-lights was much more difficult with this object than it was in figure 4.7. The simpler, curved shape in figure 5.19 offers less opportunity to begin, end, or merge card and light reflections. Matte sprays can reduce or eliminate these reflec-tions. Unfortunately, they also elimi-nate the real texture of the surface and should be used sparingly.

of-sight around the object. It also mirrors all imperfections and textures, too. Backdrop paper couldn't be used in this case because the paper's texture would be easily detectable as a reflection on the object.

It is generally not a good idea to use commercially available matte sprays to reduce reflectivity on any art object like this. The effect is not only quite obvious, but typically eliminates the feel of the surface altogether. Nothing will look glossy and slick. Unless you run this liquid through an airbrush, light coats don't come out very even. The semidrying matte sprays can leave a hard-to-remove residue on some surfaces and may ruin the piece.

I used a medium gray formica background, since its surface has negligible texture. The gray surface reflected onto the bot-tom curve in the object, making this area a bit lighter in tone, which reproduced nicely in the photograph. A white back-ground surface would make this same area lighter, but its reflec-tion and outline would be much more obvious—something that I try to avoid.

Initially, the main light's reflection on top of the teapot had an awkward shape. I moved the main overhead light up and down, forward and back until its reflection on the teapot had a more pleasing shape. One large white matte fill card (30 × 40 inches), placed at a 45-degree angle to the teapot, created the

Figure 5.20. Ceramic teapot, Adrianne Saxe, 1990. The "feet" of this teapot are buried under the main structure. White reflectors had little effect on this heavy shadow area. Silver reflector cards were necessary to lighten the teapot's "feet" enough to see them clearly. The irregular shape of this object in combination with the pattern in the glaze itself made lighting easier than in figure 5.19.

reflection on its left. The fill card had to sit evenly on the table and be tall enough to be snug against the main light's edge. Any gap at the top or bottom would reflect as a thin dark line between much lighter reflections. I was trying to make these reflection blend in as much as possible.

One more 30 × 40-inch white matte card was cut to size to allow just enough clearance for its position directly beneath the lens. This card's angle was adjusted to produce a slightly brighter reflection than the card to the left. Having one slightly brighter reflection next to another provides a visual logic for the two adjacent areas, as if there were another light source off in the distance. It also adds another shade to the limited palette of this monotone subject. Silver reflector cards could not be used since most have a slight pebble texture that makes itself apparent in reflections on shiny pieces like this.

The silver-toned glaze in the Adrianne Saxe ceramic piece (figure 5.20) is another example of a highly reflective surface. This photo was taken on location at a gallery, so I didn't have as wide an assortment of reflector materials available as I do in the studio. Nonetheless, I still needed to create the best looking reflections possible. The slight texture on this ceramic piece breaks up the hard-edged reflection enough to allow me to use one of the shiny pebble silver cards as a reflector on each side.

The extra light I was able to create by using silver reflector cards produced enough fill light to accurately depict the base of the piece. I needed the silver cards because the white matte cards left the base a few shades darker. I wiggled the silver cards around until I saw the light effects I wanted, then I secured the cards in that position. My concern centered on the shape and placement of the obvious darker spots on the front of the object, which were the reflection of the darkened room. I could not, nor did I want to, eliminate these entirely.

I did not want regularly shaped (square, rectangular, etc.) reflections because the shape of the lighting would become too obvious and would contrast too much with the slightly irregular shape of the piece itself. The dark areas are scattered and skewed enough that they don't dominate the piece. Had I been in my studio, I would have lightened this dark area using a technique described in the discussion of shooting behind glass (page 43). I would hang a light to medium gray 9-inch-wide backdrop near the camera to reflect into the dark areas of the piece and raise the illumination enough to lighten it a few shades.

Although I have used ceramic examples, the same rules apply to glass, metal, plastic, or anything else that inherently makes mirrorlike reflections.

Glassware

Shooting glassware and other transparent or translucent objects requires a different approach than anything else covered in this book. Instead of having a main light illuminating the outside of an object, we need to have a highly controlled main light passing through the object. For most opaque objects, fill cards are added to increase detail in shadow areas. For translucent or transparent objects such as a wine glass, cards are often used to create dark reflections on the object that give it form and shape.

The easiest way to shoot glassware is on a light table. Figure 5.24C (page 118) shows a professional model that is designed to hold a 4 x 8-foot piece of plexiglass up to ⅜-inch thick. A light head placed underneath or just behind the plexi becomes the main light source.

Beautiful and elegant results can be created with one light head below the table aimed just in front of or slightly behind the glass object's position. The light often needs to have some diffusion, even though it is eventually going to shine through plexi or another material that diffuses it further. Raw light from a lamp doesn't have very far to travel underneath a light table and will generally produce an unattractive, small hot spot. A diffuser attached to the light head softens the hot spot and spreads the light over a larger area with a smoother gradient. This doubled diffusion won't lead to longer exposures or the need to go to more powerful lights. The distances from light to plexi are usually quite close, and the object is literally sitting on a lit surface. Lamps of even moderate output allow for very small apertures.

Figure 5.21 is an example of another diffuser made by simply bouncing the light off a large white piece of matte board placed on the floor beneath the table. This creates a nice glow that fades very gradually with no apparent hot spots. Changing the light head's angle will create infinite variations in highlight placement and the speed of light gradation.

As with many glassware shots, a careful placement of the main light is often all that is needed to finish the lighting. Quite often, no reflectors or fill cards are necessary at all. (If you ever get stuck after adding several cards to a glassware shot, take them all out and look again!) I did this photo on location in a storage area at a museum that was a fortuitously large area with black walls and ceilings. This black working area eliminated the likelihood of anything in the environment being reflected on the glassware itself.

Professionals who photograph a lot of glassware will often build their studio just like this, and will also paint the floor black and buy black equipment (stands, cameras, tripods, etc). Any reflection will then be of the photographer's own making.

For the rest of us, who are without access to such ideal set-

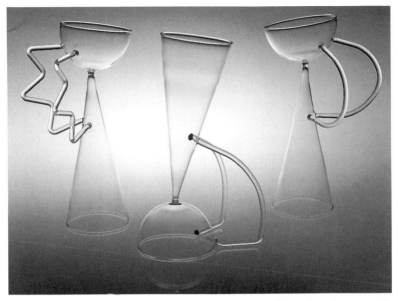

Figure 5.21. The elegant lighting seen here consists of just one well-placed light bouncing off a white card beneath a light table. Slight changes in the light's position will create a wide variety of effects.

tings, it often becomes necessary to specifically block the reflections with a black card or paper and create a temporary set that is photographically neutral. I often had to hang a piece of black backdrop paper high over the set to eliminate the reflection in the curve of the plexi or the sprinkler system in my studio. A matte-surfaced white plexi could have been used in this circumstance (or matte spray applied), but I personally like the visual effect of the hard-edged reflections created by the smooth plexi.

Any light that is placed underneath the table usually reflects some of the floor's color onto the back side of the table. If you have wooden floors, this means the plexi will probably have a brownish cast in the photo. The easiest way to correct this is to completely cover the area beneath the table with black or white backdrop paper, or anything else that is similarly neutral. If you are using sawhorses as supports, paint them black or

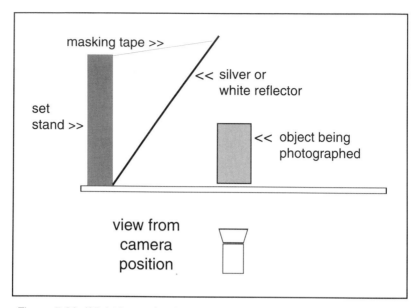

Figure 5.22. If light is coming from beneath the surface, fill cards need to be angled *down*, as illustrated, to reflect light toward an object on the surface.

white because they, too, can create an unwanted cast if you aren't careful.

When new, most commercially available white plexi and other white diffusion materials inherently produce photographic results that have a slight but distinct coolish cast, which I prefer. As the material is aged by heat and other environmental factors, I begin adding blue filtration as needed to keep the gray areas slightly cool. This can also be accomplished by placing a light blue backdrop paper underneath the table instead of a neutral color. Going one step farther, if you bounce a light off a dark blue paper, it will produce a very distinctive blue cast in the region where it hits the plexi. I've used this technique to add any overall color I wanted to the photograph. For example, in a two-light situation you can have one color in the upward curve of the sweep (the top of the frame or the background), and another color (or neutral) in the foreground.

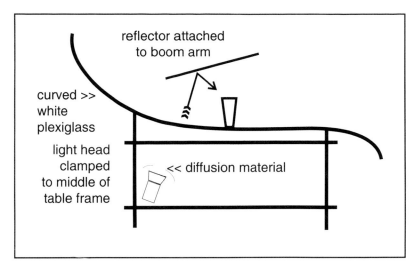

Figure 5.23. This illustration shows the principle involved in top reflectors placement to create highlights around the top edge of the object, similar to the highlights created by the main light in previous examples.

When reflective fill cards are needed in a setup with under lighting, the card has to be angled down toward the light source in order to be reflected (see figure 5.22). A long piece of tape attached to the top of the reflector will hold the card in position so you can adjust it as necessary. Another way to hold a reflector is to use a boom arm. Figure 5.23 shows a fill card in position above (not touching) the setup to reflect light from the table back at the object. Use A-clamps or tape to secure the reflector to the boom arm. Adjustment of the intensity and direction of reflected light is accomplished by rotating the boom arm (see page 87).

It is always very useful to have black matte card on hand if you want to create darker reflection in some clear glass pieces. At best, white cards produce light gray reflections that may not be dark enough to achieve the effect you need, such as adding a very dark edge to replace one that appears white on the set. The same black reflection often appears several times again in the interior of glassware, adding both density and punch to

Figure 5.24A, B. Multicolored glass goblet by Josh Simpson, Santa Fe series, 1979. The front of this translucent goblet has one pattern, the rear another. The pattern seen in the photograph is a combination of the two. Rotating the glass produces an infinite variety of patterns. Have an assistant turn the glass so that you can observe the pattern changes.

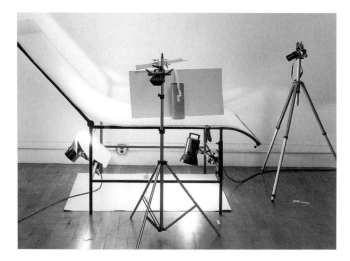

Figure 5.24C. Side view of light table and lighting used to photograph figures 5.24 A, B.

inherently low-contrast objects. When black cards can't be used or don't create the effect I want, I sometimes resort to drawing edges on the object with a black grease pencil or sticking black tape strategically on it to create dark edges on clear pieces that would otherwise disappear into the background. This technique is very easy to control, and you can easily remove pencil or tape marks from any pieces that you can safely apply glass cleaner to. If you are in doubt about marking the surface of a piece, don't use this technique.

Of course, you don't need a professional light table to shoot glassware, and you can easily make one that fits your specific needs. For years I used a thin sheet of plexi with the curved end taped to a wall and the sides held up by long sawhorses. Before that, I used a large sheet of glass on sawhorses draped with a roll of tracing vellum or any similar translucent material on top as the diffusion material. However you make your table, be sure that it is stable since most glassware is extremely fragile.

Variations

To photograph some glass objects, two lights will often be needed to get the effect wanted. This is especially true of glassware that is relatively dark, like Josh Simpson's piece in figures 5.24A and B. One light was aimed just in front of the stem to illuminate the front surface, while the other light was placed directly behind it to pass strong light through the glass and reveal that it was indeed translucent.

I had to rotate the glass incrementally to try to find the most

Figure 5.25A. The same multi-colored brown goblet used in figure 5.24. I used strong side-lighting to create this variation.

Figure 5.25B. The same set-up as Figure 5.25A, photo-graphed with a 35mm camera.

pleasing angle, which proved to be quite difficult. I ended up shooting several shots in various positions because the combination of effects produced on the glass varied so dramatically.

I did another variation of this piece that focused more heavily on the saturated colors in the glass (figures 5.25A–B). A strong sidelight directed at the piece provided the main light, while a second light illuminated the gradated background some distance behind the glass. Although it is a dramatic photograph, it does not suggest that the glass is translucent. You can make your own decisions about which procedure to use to best represent your particular glassware piece.

Fabrics, Rugs, Paper, and Other Low-Contrast Matte Objects

There are many objects that require lighting that emphasizes their texture above all else. Refer to figure 4.14A on page 78. It shows a small matte white sculpture. If you were to photograph this using highly diffused light, little of the surface texture could be seen. Using an umbrella with a silver mylar lining punched up the contrast. Since the light is more directional, the shadow areas become darker and better defined, showing a lot more of the "roughness" of the surface.

A similar object that was matte black, gray, white, or any other monotone would be enhanced by increasing the contrast of the light, or by changing the direction of the light in such a manner that would emphasize surface texture. Figure 5.26A shows a rough-textured rug with lighting from a 45-degree angle to the lens axis. Notice that there seems to be little texture in the paper. Figure 5.26B has the light at an 80-degree angle, and the actual texture is quite apparent. A fill card on the opposite side of the light can be used to control precisely the depth of the shadows.

Photographs of most rugs, tapestries, weavings, papers, paper origami, textiles, and other art that is basically flat will all benefit in a similar way when you use direct sidelighting. You can also get wonderful effects from a few well placed raw light sources. Keep in mind, however, that most viewers are more interested in seeing the object rather than the lighting, however spectacular it may be.

Large rugs, weavings, and tapestries are easier to photograph if hung flat on a wall. Begin by placing the lights close to the wall, but all to one side of the object, to emphasize its texture. Use as many lights as needed to give the impression that a large light source is shining from that direction. Adjust the distance of the light from the wall as needed to obtain the surface texture you desire. Add fill reflectors on the opposite side, or additional lights, if there is too much light fall-off occurring from one side to the other due simply to the distance of object from light source. (This is the inverse square law: double the distance from a light source and the light intensity will diminish by a factor of four. Photographically this equals a two-stop change in light meter readings.) If the object is very large and complicated, be sure to get in close and do a number of detail shots.

Photos of paper sculptures that are not essentially flat objects will benefit when you use a more directional and contrast-producing lighting—a box light or a silver bounce umbrella, for example. Many of the three-dimensional pieces that I have

Figure 5.26A. Detail shot of a Navajo rug with the lighting placed at a 45-degree angle to the rug's surface.

Figure 5.26B. The light for this shot was lowered until it was only 15 degrees up from the plane of the rug so that the surface texture could be emphasized.

photographed are partially translucent and look best when shot on a light table in the same fashion as glassware. You may even want to explore this method first with some completely opaque sculptures.

Very Large Objects

Photographing large art objects often poses no more difficulty than photographing smaller ones. The only difference is the size of the backdrop and reflector cards used. For example, a 2- or a 6-foot-high bronze statue can probably be photographed using the same basic lighting equipment. While the smaller one will fit nicely on a 54-inch-wide backdrop, the larger would need a 108- or 144-inch backdrop for a perfect seamless sweep. You will probably use 30 × 30-inch and smaller reflectors to photograph the 2-foot-high sculpture, while the larger one might require 4 × 8-foot reflectors that photographers call *flats*.

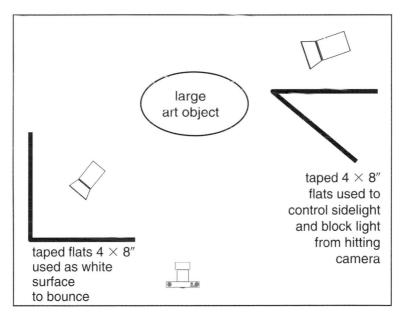

large art object

taped 4 × 8″ flats used to control sidelight and block light from hitting camera

taped flats 4 × 8″ used as white surface to bounce

Figure 5.27A. Useful lighting and flat configurations for photographing large objects, top view.

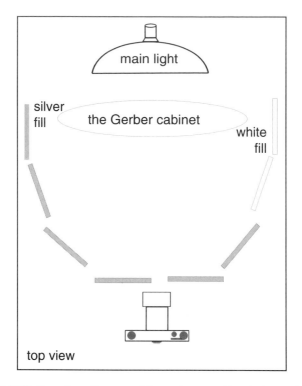

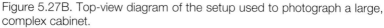

Figure 5.27B. Top-view diagram of the setup used to photograph a large, complex cabinet.

Most art supply houses or framing shops keep in stock or can order foam core of various thicknesses for you. Thinner pieces of foam core work well individually as simple reflectors, whereas the thicker ones can be taped together on their 8-foot-long side so that they can stand alone (see figure 5.27A). So taped, they can be configured in many ways and shapes to bounce or block light as needed. These reflectors will provide nice, broad reflections in shiny objects or supply the needed fill to boost shadow detail as mentioned in chapter 3.

Figure 5.27B shows another approach to photographing large objects. I used several smaller 30 × 40-inch reflectors to shoot this 66-inch-wide object. Each one was carefully positioned and adjusted to create numerous small highlights, bringing out the

Figure 5.27C. The Gerber Cabinet by Tod Granzow, 1992. Multiple reflector cards created the numerous highlights that were needed to define the many curves and elements that make up this cabinet.

subtleties of the complex and elegant Gerber Cabinet (figure 5.27C) designed and produced by Tod Granzow of Santa Fe, New Mexico. Photographing a large-scale piece such as this one enables us to have extremely fine image control that would be quite difficult on a smaller object.

Imagine this piece smaller by a factor of six, which would make it 11 inches wide. Controlling that many small reflectors in a limited area is akin to stacking a deck of cards. It becomes too easy for them to knock into one another. Card adjustments for the original version often involved movements of mere millimeters to induce slight curvature. This would be nearly impossible to do when photographing the reduced version of this cabinet.

This shot required about four hours to set up on location, half of which time was spent adjusting reflectors to achieve these results. Fortunately, the designer was on set during that time to point out all the features and elements that make this very complex cabinet special. This reinforces my opinion that the artist who creates the work is most often the best qualified person to

Figure 5.27D. The cabinet top was removed so that it could be photographed on the same set. The reflector cards were adjusted or changed as needed.

create an interpretive photo of his or her art. The next best thing would be for the artist to closely supervise a skilled photographer, especially when dealing with a complex object like this one.

We also photographed several details as well as a shot of the top of the piece (figure 5.27D). The combination of figures 5.27C and D gives a very complete picture of the unique curvaceous shape of the cabinet. Fortunately, this cabinet was in the final stage of completion and the top had not been permanently attached. It was easier to shoot this by itself than to execute an "aerial" view, which would require a 15-foot-high tripod and ladder, or a high balcony that has wide-open space below (no supports or other obstructions). Such an aerial view would also require a 20-foot-high ceiling. Unless you have access to work space and equipment to execute an aerial view of this proportion, it will become necessary to scout for a suitable location to rent or to figure out a way to shoot the object on its side, like I did.

6

Jewelry and Close-up Photography

Coping with the Small Things in Life

I've probably spent half of my professional life shooting jewelry and other small-product ads, some of which involved pretty spectacular special effects. Most of the photographers I know consider photographing jewelry and extreme close-ups the most difficult assignments they can take on. It takes a light touch, fine motor skills, patience, and tremendous attention to detail to get really good jewelry photos. As jewelers and artists, you have developed these skills and qualities but will need to learn a few specific techniques for photographing jewelry and other small objects. Many of these skills involve various methods for positioning and displaying the art. But first you need to understand the most important part of the process: close-up photography and equipment.

Special Equipment
Macro Lenses

Unless your photographic assignments are limited to large necklaces, you will more than likely need a special close-up lens or a set of extension rings that enable you to focus closely on an object (figure 6.1). You will need to photograph pins,

Figure 6.1. Macro lenses. *Top* 55mm macro with life-size adaptor. *Bottom* 105mm macro with lens hood attached, life-size adaptor to right.

bracelets, and broaches at about one-half life-size on 35mm film. Rings should be photographed almost life-size to fill the 35mm frame adequately. The standard lenses that you may already own will only reproduce about one-seventh to one-tenth life size on film.

The best and easiest approach is to use the specialized close-up lenses, usually referred to as macro or micro lenses. Macro lenses are generally designed for life-size reproduction or smaller; micro lenses are designed for life size and larger, and are capable of magnifying the image size several times life-size on film. By simply twisting the focus on most macro lenses, you can go continuously from infinity (for distant objects such as mountains) to one-half life-size. Add the manufacturer's matched extension ring to its spedific macro lens to go from one-half life-size to life-size. These lenses usually have a smaller maximum aperture and are specifically optimized and corrected for the near side of the focusing range (the ones in figure 6.1 are optimized for one-fourth life-size). At its optimum range, a macro lens produces incredibly sharp images, usually the best in each camera manufacturer's lineup of lenses. These same lenses don't perform as well when focused on distant objects, but are comparable to other lenses of the similar focal length.

The macro lens optical design is relatively simple, usually

having fewer lens elements than the normal lens that came with your camera. The high cost of these lenses stems mainly from the low volume of production. The manufacturer might make 25,000 normal lenses per year and only 500 macro lenses. The per-unit production cost is so low for the high-volume normal lenses the manufacturers often *give* them to dealers as a bonus for buying a certain number of camera bodies.

Macro lenses come in different focal lengths, from 50mm to 300mm. I have personally used the most popular and inexpensive macro focal length, either a 55mm or 60mm, as a dual-purpose lens, forgoing altogether the 50mm lens of normal design. When focused at life-size, or slightly smaller, the end of the of a 55mm lens is only a few inches away from the object. While this is workable, it can impose a few restrictions in lighting and reflector placement, as well as physical inconvenience in viewing (typically bending over the set supported only by your back).

A 100mm-focal-length macro lens will allow twice the distance (for any given reproduction ratio) between the camera and the object, and provides a more comfortable working environment. Unfortunately, most manufacturers charge two to three times as much for a 100mm lens (produced in very limited quantities), compared to their more popular macro lens in the 50mm to 60mm range. If most of your photos need near life-size reproduction, a 100mm macro is the best choice if you can afford it.

Many manufacturers now make macro zoom lenses that offer very limited close-up capabilities. Most of these types have one fixed macro setting—about one-third life-size—with little or no focusing ability. Focus is achieved by moving the camera in and out until the image is sharp. Unless you already own a lens of this type, don't even bother to look at one. If you do own one, try photographing a typical art piece and make sure that you are not severely restricted by using this type of lens exclusively. Though some of these lenses are quite good optically, to use them is usually a compromise. You will achieve much better results with the simple five- or six-element fixed-focal-length macro lenses than with the complicated twelve- to eighteen-element zoom lens with limited macro capability. Going through that many lenses is never a good thing, even with optical glass as good as it is today. The degradation is not obvious, but subtle, revealing itself in lower levels of overall contrast and color saturation. In addition, zoom lenses may come close, but generally never achieve the image quality of any fixed-focal-length lenses (by the same manufacturer) within the zoom's range. Because of the magnification factor, close-up photography makes any lens defect all the more apparent.

Buying a new lens isn't the only option for having good equipment. Used macro lenses can be bought for about one-half to two-thirds the cost of a new lens. Most manufacturers still play the horsepower game a bit, trying to make faster and faster lenses. Older model lenses may have a one-half or one full stop smaller maximum aperture, so the image will be slightly dimmer seen through the viewfinder. At typical shooting apertures for close-up work, f11–22, there is hardly any difference, if at all, between macro lenses of the same manufacturer in the last twenty years.

When buying a used lens, carefully check the mechanical operation of all its moving parts. If the lens is in very good shape cosmetically, the owner obviously took care of it or didn't use it very much, which is a definite plus. Since these are special-purpose lenses, chances are they received little use. Never buy a lens that looks abused or appears to have been dropped. Try to buy from a store or private owner who will allow you to do some test shots before purchase or give you a cash refund if you are not satisfied. Some stores will rent you the particular lens for about $10 a day for testing purposes and then refund this fee on purchase.

It may be more cost effective for you to just rent any specialty lens when needed. Weekly rates are about three times as high as the daily rates. If you arrange to shoot your work along with other photographers, you can split the rental costs.

Extension Tubes

Another way to photograph objects close-up is to add extension tubes between your normal or short telephoto lens and the camera body. Lenses with smaller maximum apertures (f2 for normal-focal-length lenses, f2.8 for telephoto) and simpler optical designs work best with extension tubes. Some optical quality is sacrificed since these lenses weren't designed to be used at such large reproduction ratios. How much loss in quality will vary with lens design and image magnification.

Some of the combinations will deliver image quality very close to that possible with macro lenses, while another combination may deliver relatively poor results. You will be able to determine if the photographic results are adequate only after testing each combination of lens and magnification you are most likely to use. If possible, borrow or rent a macro lens and test it at the same time so that you can have a direct comparison.

Extension tubes come in sets of various extensions to be used individually or in combination to vary the reproduction ratio. Tubes aren't as convenient to use as lenses because they require more handling than simply twisting a focusing ring. However, if you are on a budget, this inconvenience might be offset by the savings in the purchase price of the tubes when compared to that of a macro lens, which is two to four times higher. And, if you shoot mostly at one specific reproduction size, you won't be inconvenienced by having to make extra adjustments when doing the photography.

Close-up Filters

Like macro-zoom lenses, unless you already own a set of these filters, this option need not be investigated. A high-quality filter set will cost you more than an extension tube set and won't work as well. Usually there are three filters per set, each allowing a different closer focusing range. Used individually, these filters work reasonably well. However, if you layer them together to achieve a greater reproduction size, the photographic results range from poor to awful.

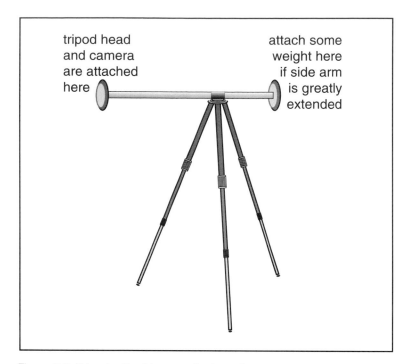

tripod head
and camera
are attached
here

attach some
weight here
if side arm
is greatly
extended

Figure 6.2. Tripod with side-arm attachment.

Tripods

A decent tripod is a necessity for close-up work. Any movement or vibration will be magnified because of the higher image reproduction ratios. Depending on the type of work involved and the focal length of the lens, a tripod that has a side-arm attachment (figure 6.2) is the best one for you to use. This arm helps extend the camera horizontally over the photographic set to position the lens at its working height and angle.

If your tripod doesn't have this accessory or if the price is out of your budget, you can extend the tripod legs to different lengths to move it close to a vertical position. I attach a heavy weight toward the end of the longest leg to keep the camera from tipping over and causing a very expensive but easily avoidable mistake.

Water Weights

Any tripod can be made more stable and inert by hanging extra weight on the center column. On location, I drape my camera bag's strap just below the base of the tripod head, adding about fifteen pounds of weight. In my studio, I use homemade water weights of gallon-sized plastic milk containers filled with water or sand; these weigh about six pounds each. I loop a few feet of nylon rope through the built-in handle so that I can hang the weight at any convenient place on the tripod.

Lighting Equipment

Most jewelry and small objects can be shot using one light source, some diffusion material, and an assortment of small cardboard reflectors. Figure 6.3 shows the setup that I use for almost all small artifacts. It may be much larger than you need, but you can create the setup that suits your own work. I rested a 3 × 4-foot plywood tabletop on three or four milk crates. A portable backdrop stand supports a 3 × 4-foot plexi at approximately a 45-degree angle. You can also make your own plexi supports from wood and attach them directly to the plywood; just be sure to provide for some vertical adjustment to allow some change in the plexi angle. If you make the

Figure 6.3. A two-tungsten-light close-up set. Note that one light is directly over the other. A clear dustcover from a defunct turntable is used to protect the set's surface and objects while the film is processed.

supports yourself, the total material cost for this setup will be about $35.

An alternative to using plexi is to buy or make a light frame (see page 84), which works just as well most of the time. Problems may arise when you are shooting objects on smooth, reflective surfaces because any ripple, texture, smudge, or similar imperfection of the diffusion material will be clearly reflected on the background or on the object itself if that, too, is highly reflective. When shooting at one-half life-size, these imperfections can look quite large. White plexi diffusion always looks smooth and perfect as long as there are no major scratches on the side facing the objects (if there are, this can be remedied by flipping the plexi over) or streaks and smudges on the surface (which a little cleaning fluid and elbow grease will eliminate).

The height of the platform in figure 6.3 allows you to stand up while shooting. You can make all adjustments by sitting on another milk crate or low stool. You may need to stand on a crate or stool if you a need bit of extra height to look through the camera viewfinder.

The rest of this chapter has specific examples and descriptions involving jewelry. However, the lighting and working techniques described here are equally applicable to all close-up photography of small objects such as fountain pens, coins, eyeglasses, flowers, and so forth. Even if you are not involved with jewelry per se, you can easily learn the photo basics and other valuable information by reading the rest of this chapter carefully while keeping your type of objects in mind.

Photographing Rings

Rings can be the most difficult objects in the world to photograph when you don't know how. You must have a very deft hand and pay close attention to small details. Before I learned what to do, I used to avoid certain clients who needed this type of photography. Then one day a new client came by with some rings for me to shoot for an ad and I watched him set up. He didn't have time to draw a layout for me, so he styled the

Figure 6.4A. Gold wedding bands by Arlyn, Cold Springs, New York, 1991. This typical jewelry shot is simple in design yet effectively exhibits the design and structure of both rings. However, the setup is complex and an illusion is needed to create this image.

Figure 6.4B. A precision ruler in the frame area accurately records the object's scale.

ad on the set, making it up as we went. I learned as I watched him and it became all so apparent. It can be that easy for you as well.

The photograph of the two rings in figure 6.4 (designed by Arlyn of Cold Spring, New York) was pretty typical and shows all the necessary elements: a simple but elegant background, reflections that show another view of the rings, tack-sharp features, highlights that add to the tactile quality of the photo, and an interesting, eye-catching composition that creates visual appeal while it shows all important aspects of the rings.

Waxing and Adjusting

Figure 6.5A shows a side view of figure 6.4. Notice that the rings are held in position at this unnatural angle by jewelers wax placed underneath each one. The camera in figure 6.5B is pulled back even farther to show the angle of the rings in relation to the camera lens.

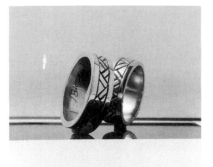

Figure 6.5A. This close-up side view shows the ring angle needed to create the illusion in Figure 6.4.

Figure 6.6 reveals how the wax was applied to the back of the rings. On wide rings, a round blob of wax can be positioned toward the front of the ring. The ring at the bottom of the photo shows how wax is applied to thinner rings. Prepare the wax by rolling a small blob between your forefinger and thumb until it is about half as thin as the ring (note the wax just to the left of the ring at the bottom). Then lightly press the wax onto the back of the ring. Now the ring is ready to be positioned on the set.

This wax adheres nicely to the plexi surface and if you look closely at the earlier photo (figure 6.5A) the ring never touches the surface. The real beauty of the wax is that once you get it stuck to the surface, you can adjust the other end of the ring several degrees. Having this adjustment capability is one of the advantages of using wax, helping to speed up the photography process. Other adhesives aren't as adjustable.

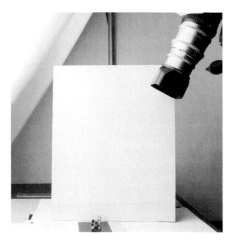

Figure 6.5B. This photo exhibits the relationship between the rings and camera angle. Note the overall size of the set, which proportionally must be much larger than sets used for larger three-dimensional objects.

Hot Glue

Hot glue can also be used to hold a ring in position, but is in general quite a bit more difficult to control than wax. Its advantage over wax is that it can hold objects at extreme angles with very little material. It takes just a very small dab of glue to be effective, but it must be placed precisely in position where the jewelry makes contact with the surface. I follow two distinct steps when using hot glue: I first dab the glue on the ring and let it solidify, cutting off any excess as needed. With a lit candle or lighter, I briefly heat up the glue by holding it near but not in the flame, then quickly place the ring into position.

You will only have two to four seconds to place the ring before the glue solidifies. If it is not in exactly the correct position, you will probably have to pull it off completely and start over because little or no adjustment is possible. Most of the time the glue will come off very cleanly or leave just a little mark on smooth, hard backgrounds. If the mark is small or can be easily covered, use it as a position marker to hit on your next attempt. When you remove it from the set try to keep the glue on the jewelry so that all you have to do is reheat and reapply.

The Proper Work Area and Supplies

I suggest making a few trial runs waxing rings and adhering them to different surfaces before you bring out the photo

Figure 6.6. This photo shows the wax shape and positioning used in figure 6.4. Note the size of "insignificant" dust left of the ring at the bottom.

equipment. A little practice in a relaxed atmosphere will build the skills and confidence needed to be cool under the hot lights and time pressure of the photo shoot. Many jewelry photographers work this way as a rule. They set up all the shots on individual background boards that are then moved in and out of the lighting setup.

Clear a flat work area big enough to spread your elbows out comfortably. Sitting at a desktop or workbench is fine, although I find an adjustable drafting table to be ideal. Even lighting from a lamp positioned in front of you at eye level (aimed at the tabletop) will help point out any imperfections in your initial setup that would ruin the final image.

Using a gooseneck or other adjustable-angle work lamp will enable you to explore different lighting angles before you place the rings into the photo set. Observe the effects of light coming from a very high and a very low position. A higher light provides a broad, even illumination while foreshortening and opening up shadow areas. Placed at the same distance from the object, a lower light looks more dramatic, makes longer shadows, and emphasizes the surface texture of the background. Make a note on what looks best with each particular ring and background combination so that you can further explore your options when preparing the photo lighting.

Before you start, try to have the following list of necessary items and supplies on hand:

1. Jeweler's wax
2. White cotton gloves and/or plastic gloves
3. Isopropyl (rubbing) alcohol or rubber cement thinner
4. Q-tips
5. Various sized tweezers
6. Small matte knife
7. Jewelry cloth and cleaner
8. Acetone
9. Matches or propane lighter

10. Canned air or large bulb ear syringe

11. Several camel hair brushes, small to large

12. Tissues and paper towels

13. Small precision ruler

Keeping It Clean
Phase One

Practice first on a smooth, durable surface such as formica or a piece of glass. These surfaces don't scratch easily and are not likely to be affected by most cleaning solvents. Tape or otherwise secure any background surfaces to keep them in position on the work table. Select and clean your rings. For convenience and organization, arrange them from the widest to the narrowest.

Using your bare hands, dig out a small chunk of the wax with your fingernail and roll it between your fingers into the shape shown at the bottom left in figure 6.6. If the shape is too large or uneven, continue rolling the wax between your forefinger and the surface until it's the right thickness and is evenly shaped.

Select a ring the width of which you think would work well with this formed piece of wax. Hold the top of the ring between your thumb and forefinger. Press the rolled wax into firm contact with the bottom of the ring all along the length (figure 6.6) with the other hand while trying not to touch any other part of the ring.

Gently push the ring where the wax is attached onto the surface in a nearly vertical position, with any design or stone centered left to right. If you didn't push quite hard enough, the ring will fall over. Just pick it up and try again with a little more pressure until it holds firmly. If you push too hard, the wax will flatten out too much, or may be pushed into clear view, something you should try to avoid.

Once the ring is suitably stuck, try changing its angle and roll it in small increments. I find it easiest to use my forefinger on the ring while I rest my fingers on the background for added stability. If you have done the previous steps correctly, you should be able to roll the ring about 10 to15 degrees to each side and 10 to 20 degrees up and down before it falls over. This is usually more adjustment than you need to do to achieve optimum alignment with the lens angle.

After you have finished practicing, scrape the wax off the background and the bottom of the ring with your fingernail. You can reuse the wax several times before it loses its adhesive qualities. If the wax in the first attempt didn't adequately hold the ring, add a little more before reforming. If there was too much wax, remove a little and try again.

Before reapplying wax to the band, clean the back of the band of any remaining wax or residue from the first attempt. Use a paper towel or tissue instead of a jeweler's cloth unless you don't mind throwing it away after each session. Repeat the whole process with all of your practice rings until you can predictably place the ring where you want it, at the angle you want, and make it stick with little if any wax visible from the camera angle.

The real trick is to initially place the ring as close to the expected best angle with the right amount of roll. This is especially important when trying to put several rings into one shot, where several adjustments to each ring becomes the rule rather than the exception. The more you fiddle with each ring, the more likely it is to fall down. I generally leave the rings in position on the background until I have my final film back, and that can be days for complicated layouts.

While you are practicing, carefully observe the area right around the stone setting for hairs and dirt, or lint from your cotton gloves. These foreign items will look incredibly large in your photo. Practice removing them with tweezers or picks while the ring is on the set, which most often is simpler to do than removing the ring altogether and starting over. If you can't remove it, try burning them off with a lighter with its flame set to extend about an inch. Just quickly pass the flame over the affected area and you will avoid scorching the jewelry (which easily wipes off most jewelry, but you will want to take the ring off the set to do so). Almost any amount of direct flame is enough to incinerate hair or lint and literally make it disappear.

Phase Two

Once you are comfortable using the wax, start with a perfectly clean ring and clean background and try to keep them that way through the entire process. Wearing thin vinyl or white cotton gloves, inspect all of your test rings for any fingerprints, residue, dirt, or hairs and clean as needed. Hold the top of each ring with your steadier hand and take the glove off your other hand to work the wax and apply it to the band.

Place each ring precisely on a predetermined spot on the background. If any wax shows or the angle of the ring is more than a few degrees off, remove that ring and start over again until each ring is perfect. Clean the background scrupulously between each attempt, since it is always easier and safer to handle this chore when the set is empty. When you feel reasonably confident and proficient at this level, it's time to put your work on film.

If you are having consistency problems, take a break and try to relax so that you can come back and work smoothly. I usually leave the set until I am in the proper frame of mind. Since I can't do this when my clients are around, I set everything up as far in advance as possible to eliminate all those deadline pressures. Besides, it's good to take a break before shooting to rest your eyes and mind. A fresh look at your set will often reveal previously unnoticed errors that must be corrected.

Shooting Your First Test Shots

The first film test is really just a shot in the dark unless you are equipped with an instant film adapter (see chapter 8, page 196). Exposure settings are a bit more difficult to pin down. If you are using a handheld incident meter, hold it just above the object and point its dome back at the camera. This meter reading is good for most general objects unless they are highly reflective, like most jewelry is. In this situation, it is best to start your exposure bracket one full stop down (smaller) in exposure. Until you gain experience working with your objects, increase the test bracket to include one full stop on either of your initial setting (see chapter 3, "The All-Important Exposure Bracket," page 50).

If the test shot's reproduction ratio is larger than 1/10th life-size, you will need to add additional exposure. If you are using specialized close-up lenses, simply find the reproduction ratio setting on the focusing ring and add corrections according to the following table. Exposure compensation is automatic if you are using your camera's through-the-lens metering. Review the section on in-camera metering on pages 41–42.

CLOSE-UP EXPOSURE CORRECTION TABLE

Reproduction ratio	Exposure increase in f-stops	Exposure factor
1/10	2/7	1.21
1/8	1/3	1.27
1/7	3/8	1.30
1/6	4/9	1.36
1/5	1/2	1.44
1/4	2/3	1.56
1/3	5/6	1.77
1/2.5	1	1.96
1/2	1-1/6	2.25
1/1.5	1-4/9	2.75
1/1	2	4.00

Don't expect your first test to produce professionally perfect photos. Once we see and analyze the test photos, we can begin to predict and control the results of the next photos. After correcting the variables in the test shot, any other object shot in the same lighting and on a similar background will have consistently perfect exposures and color balance.

Figure 6.7. A one-light close-up set.

Try out a number of backgrounds in the lighting to see which one works best with the small objects you are photographing. Simple, neutral-colored backgrounds work well in a wide variety of situations and don't compete with the art for the viewer's attention. It's important that the object visually separates from the background in both color and shade. Usually, the more the object stands out against the background the better.

The same goes for lighting. An object that is evenly lit with a broad, diffuse light source is usually a more representative depiction of the art than a photo that is dramatically lit. When photographing artwork, my goal is always to help the viewer see the art, not the photography.

I suggest that you start with the light source far enough away from your diffusion material to allow the light to spread enough to cover most of the surface (see figure 6.7). Place or build your set roughly in the center of the table and observe what happens as you move it both toward and away from the light source. Select the position that you like the most.

While handholding the camera, focus and frame the area to be photographed. Note the height and distance you are from the object and set up the tripod to hold the camera in that position. If the object is very small, such as a ring or pin, I find it much easier to preset the focus to a specific reproduction ratio (usually right on the focusing ring of macro lenses) and move the camera until the image is sharp. If the image is too large or too small for the frame, change the reproduction ratio accordingly and repeat. This will only take a few seconds. I have clients and friends who stubbornly refuse to do this. They twist and turn my focusing rings for minutes, get frustrated, and hand the camera back to me. I preset the lens, tell them not to touch the focus and three seconds later have the image sharp in the viewfinder.

With the camera in position and attached to the tripod, it's time to make the final adjustments on the set. This will involve much looking through the camera followed by small adjustments to the set or the items on the set. A lot of time and effort is saved with the help of an assistant. If you are jointly working on photos with another artist, he or she would be the ideal assistant. If you can, enlist the aid of someone who has very fine motor skills, but only after you have enough experience yourself to explain and direct their actions. If that is not possible, find someone with developed visual skills and have them direct you in the adjustments. I work with and train people who can do both. We switch positions often to break the routine and relieve each other.

If you are working alone, expect to move back and forth a lot between the camera or the set, which increases the likelihood of bumping the camera or moving the set. Once it is carefully positioned, tape or affix the set to the table and mark the position of the tripod legs on the floor so that it can be easily repositioned if moved. I need to resituate the camera quite often during many of my complicated shots. Once the lighting and reflectors are placed in the final position, often the only way I can get to the set for adjustments is through the camera position.

Also note that vinyl or white cotton gloves should be worn by the person making the position adjustments on the set to reduce the possibility of leaving any fingerprints or smudges on the objects. And if you are working with a single object, make sure that the image is properly centered in the viewfinder. Some cameras have optional viewfinder screens with etched grids that make this chore easy, as well as providing an accurate cross-check for any vertical and or horizontal in the picture. Always recheck the composition and framing of multiple objects before moving on.

Before proceeding to the next step, reread the section "All About Reflectors" on page 61. Everything in that section applies to close-up photography, and you should use the information here.

Making the Gems Sparkle

Now the real fun begins. Making the gems on a ring sparkle is a challenge, even for knowledgeable pros. The gem is

Figure 6.8 This was the first test shot for a jewelry ad. The more complicated the shot, the more necessary and essential it is to test the procedure. The background and its relationship with the rings had to be very
carefully calculated. This shot required four more tests before it was completed.

the predominant feature of many rings and is therefore high-
lighted in the photograph. It is especially important to define
and highlight a faceted gemstone's table (the flat, top-most surface of the stone, if it has one). The best way to accomplish this
is to find the position on your set where the gem is in the best
relation to the main light, paying particular attention to the
gem's table, then adding the necessary reflectors. Both parts of
the process often require considerable time and patience.

If you are a beginner, it is better to shoot each ring by itself
before tackling more complicated shots (see figure 6.8). This
allows you to place the reflectors in very close proximity to the
ring, giving you much greater and easier control. If other rings
are added, each adjustment of the lights, camera angle, or
reflectors affects each object in the shot, often adversely.
However, with experience, multiple ring setups are not so
daunting.

Once you have the ring positioned and looking the way you
want it in the viewfinder, you must then pay very close attention to what is happening visually in the gem itself. Are there

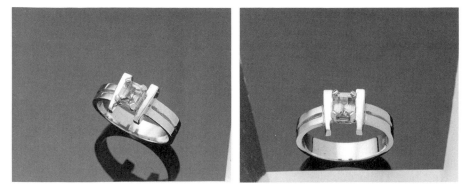

Figure 6.9A, B. These photos illustrate how a ring ellipses when photographed at an angle or straight across the frame area. The stone or design area of a horizontally oriented ring (6.9B) must be perfectly centered and balanced in relation to the camera. The angled ring (6.9A) is placed at the top of the frame so that it appears visually balanced with the photograph.

big dark areas? Are there large bright areas that show no apparent detail? Does it resemble the gem as you have pictured it in your mind? Then, if everything looks great, take a test shot and study the results by projecting the slide or using a lupe, a magnifying device that can be placed directly on the slide mount.

If the test photo doesn't meet your standards, you'll need to start making small adjustments. It is easiest to start by moving the fill cards, or changing them to silver reflectors. Looking at the setup from the camera position rather than through the lens will help you see more detail since the camera and lens combination darkens the image by at least a factor of eight. With your head in approximate camera position, observe the effects of each card's movement, or the addition or removal of other reflectors. When you see something that you like, lock the card in position and tune as you look through the viewfinder. Sometimes it takes a very large card to get the effect needed, so try all sizes. If the gems look washed out or very flat (low contrast) try removing one card at a time.

Often a reflector card is needed right at the camera position.

A dark area in the photograph is often just the reflection of the camera and the surrounding area. I have a number of different types and sizes of card with a precut circular hole slightly larger than the lens shade for just this reason. These cards are taped from the back to a dowel rod and inserted into an inexpensive clamp that allows the rod to be rotated in one plane (see figure 6.10). Precise adjustment of the reflected light is now possible.

If you are moving or adding fill cards and don't get the results needed, next try adjusting the angle of the light slightly up, down, left, or right. You may want to mark the position before doing this so that the light(s) can be easily returned to the starting point, especially if all your testing is done. Mark the position of the light stand's feet with tape or grease pencil. Also mark the position of the stand's center column. If you are using tracing vellum or plexi as diffusion, a very small piece of tape marking the hot spot of the light is extremely useful for repositioning the direction of the light precisely. Moving the light

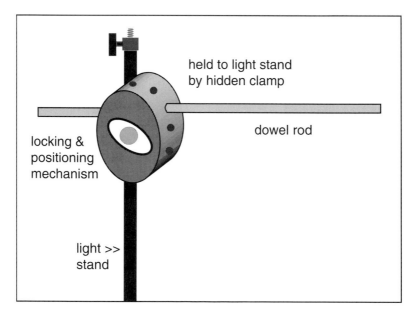

Figure 6.10. A dowel rod held by a clamp.

closer to or farther away from the diffusion material changes the contrast up or down accordingly and should be tried if the other lighting movements don't fully work.

Moving the light source will change the size, shape, and quality of the shadows and reflections. So be sure to observe all of the ramifications. Even when your gemstone sparkles, you want the rest of the shot to look good, too. If all adjustments fail to produce the image you want, return the lighting to the original position and try again with new variations and combinations.

You can also try these tricks, too, after all else has failed. First, use a small mirror rather than a card fill. Use the mirror carefully because the resulting light reflection can be very strong. Minimize this effect by placing the mirror far away, moving it closer as needed. I use small 1-inch-diameter mirrors to add little sparkles throughout multifaceted gems, like diamonds. In the business, this is known as adding "fire."

You can also accomplish this effect by poking a strategically placed hole in the diffusion material to allow some raw light to pass through directly to the gem. There is a lot of trial and error involved in this method, so be prepared to use a lot of material. You can get a similar result if you place a mirror to catch some of the raw light and reflect it precisely onto the gem in question. A larger mirror would be useful in this situation. Again, the idea is not to overpower the basic lighting in any way, but just to add the sparkle that you want.

Many rings with large stones may not have a backing directly behind the gem, so it may be necessary to create a backing with tape, paper, or foil. Experiment with each until the optimum effect is accomplished when looking at the ring in photographic light. The backing may need to be white, black, silver, or the color of the stone to be most effective.

Hoop Bracelets

Hoop bracelets can be treated like very large rings. Most look best when they are propped up with wax or hot glue, just like a ring. The biggest problem you will have is getting enough depth of field, even with the smallest of apertures such as f32 or f45 found on the specialized macro lenses. Focus precisely at one-third the distance from the very top of the hoop to the bottom to maximize depth of field (see figure 1.3). If the hoop is smooth and shiny (making it very difficult to focus on a specific point accurately) have an assistant indicate the one-third distance point with a pencil or brush while you focus on it.

If you aren't using a macro lens, shoot a test shot first using the smallest f-stop on the lens (usually f16 or f22) at the one-third focus setting and check the results. If it isn't sharp top to bottom, you have the choice of reducing the size of the hoop in the frame, or focusing closer, toward the top of the bracelet, and letting the background go a bit soft. Just make sure that the top is tack-sharp. Some amount of fuzziness elsewhere in the photo can be forgiven as long as the most important features (or at least the top) of the bracelet remain sharp and clear.

Link Necklaces and Other Bracelets

Jewelry that is not rigid, such as link necklaces or bracelets, can be laid flat on a surface singly or in groups (see figure 6.11). Care must be taken to have all the links evenly spaced and kink-free. I use a variety of different-sized camel hair brushes from 00 and up to carefully arrange and "brush" each link into place once the object is on the set. I use these brushes for

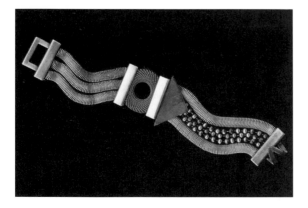

Figure 6.11. Bracelet by Jill Schwartz/Elements, 1991. The smooth "S" curves of the bracelet add movement and style to this photo. It also provides visual clues to the construction and nature of this piece of jewelry.

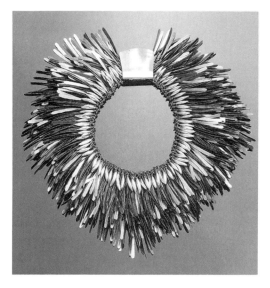

Figure 6.12. Complex jewelry and complex setups require both time and patience. Each element of this necklace had to be adjusted individually to avoid unwanted gaps and bright reflections.

nothing else so that they stay clean and will never soil or mark the surface. I also use the large brushes to clean the set of any dust a final time *just* before clicking the shutter. If you are working in a dusty environment, it may be necessary to do this before each exposure. Antistatic brushes, used for negatives in darkrooms and available at any camera store, will actually repel dust for a limited amount of time and may be a necessity under certain atmospheric conditions.

I buy brushes that have a sharp point at the end of the handle, allowing me to flip the brush around to poke or pull at things with the pointy end. Using a brush in these ways helps you create elegant shapes that can add some style to the photo. Just don't overdo the flair of your arrangement to the point where it detracts from the jewelry as the main focus of attention. Figure 6.12 shows a complicated necklace that had to be arranged very carefully. Each of its elements had to be positioned to lay together properly, then rearranged to minimize any unwanted highlights, as very bright spots always catch your attention.

This shot was also set up so that there was a gradual back-

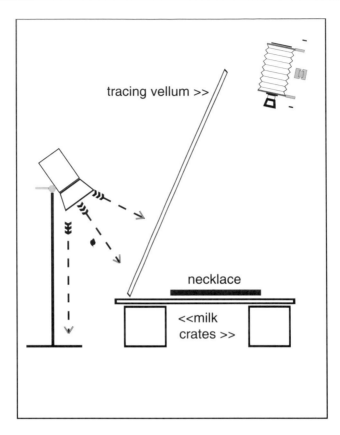

tracing vellum >>

necklace

<<milk
crates >>

Figure 6.13. Lighting diagram for figure 6.11.

ground fade from top to bottom. I accomplished this by carefully placing the light so that it fell higher than center of the necklace (see figure 6.13). The reverse (lighter at the bottom, darker
at the top) could happen if the light was directed so that it fell
lower than center. These fades work best with objects of uniform color or intensity because this lighting breaks up the composition's uniformity and adds drama.

Objects that don't work well with a light fade can be placed
on a gradated background (see figure 6.14). You can buy these
in a variety of sizes and colors at many art supply stores, or

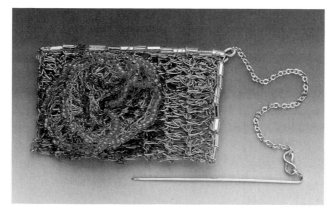

Figure 6.14. Crocheted wire pin by Arlyn, 1988. Approx. 3"w. The gradated background in this shot is readily available at most art-supply houses. The lighting can be very broad and bright since it is not being used to create fall-off in the background. This setup is very good for photographing complex or very dark objects and is also useful for quick and easy record photographs.

make them yourself using an airbrush. Either way, these surfaces tend to be fairly fragile and take little or no abuse.

On 30 × 40-inch store-bought gradated backgrounds, I start at one extreme edge and work my way across the surface until it is all used up. If you are shooting many different-sized objects, start with the smallest and work toward the largest. The larger objects will hide the blemishes created when you worked with the smaller objects.

Earrings

Earrings pose a peculiar problem if the studs are attached. Unless you bend, break, or insert them through the surface, the earrings will sit at some awkward angles. If you made the earrings and wish to photograph them, create a special set for photography and later attach the studs. If this is not possible, sometimes bending the studs carefully so that they remain hidden from the camera will work, although many I have worked with have broken off.

Another way to place them on a background is to cut small holes into the surface. When doing this, first position the earring carefully with their stems up (flipped on their back) and very precisely mark and drill the holes as small as possible. Afterwards, tape a thin sheet of styrofoam or a like material behind the background to give the stems something to adhere to and to hold them in place. These sets are very small and movable. You can create as many as needed and just place them into the lighting setup when you are finished testing, which will speed up the shooting process considerably. You can reuse many of the sets if the holes are covered strategically with larger objects.

Another special problem with earrings arises from the fact that they come in pairs and should look the same in the photograph. This can be harder than you think. I have worked with many pairs of earrings that are not equal in size. Minimize this effect by staggering them slightly in your composition.

Another problem will occur if the earrings are not sitting at precisely the same angle on the surface, resulting in a different lighting effect on each earring. Correct this by placing small bits of paper or wax under the ends of the earrings until the lighting looks exactly the same on both. Be sure to pay particular attention to the amount of glare or light fall-off on each. Use tweezers and cotton gloves to keep the jewelry clean of any oily finger smudges.

Figure 6.15 shows a pair of earrings, designed by Jill Schwartz of Elements in New York City, that needed to be adjusted in exactly this method. We photographed all of her work on a black velvet as was required for a juried show she was entering. As is often the case, the jurors wanted a plain black or white background so that the focus would be on the jewelry and not the background itself. We used black whenever possible because it looks sexier and snappier than white. For artists doing multimedia shows, the black background allows several images to be overlapped slightly without the edges of the frame showing.

Figure 6.15. Earrings by Jill Schwartz/Elements, 1991. 2½"h. Each earring had to be placed at different angles to the camera to make the lighting look the same on each. The asymmetrical composition breaks up the static quality that would result if the earrings were perfectly even and also hides the slight difference in earring length.

Miscellaneous Hints

Some necklaces that have a rigid shape looks horrible if photographed on a flat surface because of their sharp angles. A neck form or mannequin will usually solve this problem. You can also add other accessories such as scarves, blouses, and hats if you so desire. If you need to use forms often, it may be wise to buy one, but you can also borrow or rent one from a store or supply house.

Unless the clasps are special and need to be shown, there is no need to include them in the photo. Just run the ends of the bracelet or necklace outside the frame area. If the clasp is unique or special, you may want to do a detail shot that features it as large as possible in addition to an overall shot. Again, do as many detail shots as necessary to tell the whole story about every important aspect of your object.

For a complete documentation of the dimensions of a piece for your records, shoot a few extra frames with a small precision ruler clearly visible in the frame area close to the object.

This not only provides scale to the object, it furnishes useful information for insurance and reproduction purposes.

Other Backgrounds for Jewelry

When photographing rings or anything else that needs to be waxed, there are many other nonporous surfaces that work well with this adhesive besides plexiglass: photographic prints, formica, many metals, polyurethaned surfaces, finished marble, slate, plastics, and glass to name just a few. I often lay a clear, thin piece of glass or plastic over an unsuitable surface that I like, but can't work on directly. Antiglare or lightly frosted glass can supply yet another effect. You will need to use hot glue to keep rings held in position on porous sufaces, such as many woods, cork, many rocks, etc. But be careful. The glue may also damage the surface.

Necklaces, earrings, and other items that can be simply laid on flat (or nearly so) surfaces can be placed on just about anything that's appropriate. There are a wide ariety of suitable fabrics that can be stretched tautly or manipulated to create additional textures and ripples (the light will have to skim low to the surface to record the added textures). Earring stems can be pushed through most fabrics and will be held in position if a styrofoam backing is used.

7

Installations

The Art of Going Places

Shooting the gallery installation is usually a simple process, because quite often the lighting is already done for you by the gallery. This is especially true for flat artwork that is mounted on walls (see figure 7.1). If the gallery has a consistent, even wash of light on all of the pieces, all the photographer must do is figure out the color balance of the lights and add the necessary filtration (covered later in this chapter) by doing an on-site film test.

With few exceptions, the gallery's incandescent (tungsten) lights are probably in the 2500°K to 3400°K range, within easy correction range of tungsten films balanced for either 3200°K or 3400°K. Galleries with a lot of skylights or any other abundance of natural light often install 5000°K lamps balanced for daylight and could be photographed using daylight films (5000°K to 5500°K).

Either way, the general-purpose lights do not have consistent color temperature from manufacturer to manufacturer, or even batch to batch. Unlike photographic lamps that are specifically color balanced to match film, there is no color standard for bulbs in the general market, which must also be designed to have a much longer useful life. The color temperature may vary considerably between the beginning and the end of its usefulness. A rule of thumb is that the older the

Figure 7.1. Most of the objects in this photograph are behind glass. Camera position and height were carefully chosen to avoid reflection of the light sources on all glass surfaces.

lamp, the lower the color temperature will be, resulting in warmer photographs.

Be sure to first ask the person in charge of the gallery's lighting if all lamps were replaced at the same time. If so, the lighting throughout the gallery should be a consistent color temperature. It is also important to know how long ago this was done. Newer lamps need less correction, and older ones more.

The exception is the popular quartz halogen lamps used in many conventional gallery spotlights. Like photo lamps, the bulbs hold their color temperature very consistently until just before they die. A lot of them have a color temperature right around 3000°K, enabling the photographer to shoot with little or no filtration, depending on other environmental conditions like wall and floor color.

For precision, it's best to use a color temperature meter, even though they are expensive, costing at least $400, depending on features and sensitivity. Fortunately, they are popular rental items for about $15 to $25 per day at professional photo shops. Most of these meters read *incident light* (the light falling on the subject, see page 4) and give a direct readout in degrees Kelvin (°K, see page 17). For example, if the meter indicates 3200°K and you are using a 3200°K tungsten film, then no correction is needed. Some meters let you select different film types and will automatically read out the filter necessary to match the light to the film balance. Refer to the meter's manual for the proper procedures and control settings. Even with this precision and convenience, a film test is the only way to positively control all variables, including meter inaccuracy.

It is not *essential* to use a color meter, just more convenient. Color meters have only recently been available and accurate at a reasonable price. Before that, their performance was less than stellar and few people could afford them, so most photographers did without. It is still possible to get perfect results, but to do so may require more than one film test and you will need to test more options initially, therefore using more film. This task is simpler the more uniform the lighting.

It is always best to keep the color temperature of the light uniform, with no mixing. In most circumstances, this means waiting until dark to eliminate the variable of the ambient daylight in the gallery. This is usually in the gallery's best interest, too, since you won't be interfering with business hours.

Filtration

To supplement the information in this section, first familiarize yourself with the film tests and corrections sections in chapter 10, beginning with color balance (page 225), before continuing.

Unless I know that the tungsten lamps emit a warmer color temperature than the film I am using, in this case 3200°K, I treat my installation test shots like those I make in the studio. The one exception is that I shoot three complete brackets using (1) no filter, (2) CC 05 blue or 82A Wratten filter, (3) CC 10 blue or 82C Wratten filter. Since most nonphoto lamps run on the warm side, testing with these slightly bluish filters usually does the trick.

The Wratten filters have clear delineations for color temperature shifts (see "Kodak Wratten filters," page 228). An 82C shifts the color temperature exactly 400°K cooler. If the light you are using measures 2800°K, the 82C filter should give perfect color balance for a 3200°K film, since 2800°K + 400°K = 3200°K. Generally the 400°K margin proves sufficient or provides an adequate basis for guessing the right filter correction when viewing the slides on my standard light box (see page 216).

If none of your test shots look perfect and are too warm, use your Wratten filters as viewing filters by placing them on top of the best looking transparency. If more than an 82A is needed, run another film test starting with an 82A in combination with an 82B (they can be screwed into each other), thereby raising the color temperature 600°K.

CC filters are a bit harder to quantify in terms of degrees Kelvin, but work in similar fashion. In practice, test shots using a CC 05 blue and CC 10 blue filter provide enough correction for most installations. If your first test looks too warm, use your CC filters as viewing filters, and note which combination works best, making sure to add the filtration numbers together. Shoot another test if more than a CC 10 blue is needed. Your second test filtration should be CC 15 B, CC 20 B, and CC 25 B.

If the film test that used no filtration comes back too cool— this is unlikely, but it can and does happen—a different set of Wratten filters should be used. These have the designation of Wratten 81 and are slightly pinkish. The 81 filter changes the color temperature exactly 100°K warmer (reducing the color temperature 100°K), the 81A exactly 200°K warmer, and so on. When using CC filters, try the CC 05 and CC 10 yellow

Figure 7.2. Phillip Mayberry installation at Garth Clark Gallery, 1989. Only one additional light was added to the gallery's existing lighting for this installation shot to boost overall light levels, which reduced the overall contrast.

ones if your first test had a bluish cast. Use CC 05 and CC 10 magenta if the test slide has a slight greenish cast.

Additional Lighting

Many installation shots do require additional lighting, even though the gallery's lighting may appear to be perfectly acceptable. A test shot will expose the lighting deficiencies so that you can improve them in another test shot or during the actual shoot. A Polaroid test shot here would be most useful (see section on view cameras, page 196). Some 35mm cameras can accept a Polaroid adapter, as do many medium-format (120 roll film) cameras, but it's best to do it in living black-and-white since color Polaroid film is balanced for daylight and short exposures.

The most common problem you will encounter is lack of detail in shadow areas, particularly with three-dimensional objects (see "Fill Light," page 71). Figure 7.2 shows the final result of an installation shot that needed some lighting reinforcement. The sides of the white pedestals would have been extremely dark without an additional light that was bounced off the ceiling.

Although I used one powerful narrow-spread light (650-watt quartz), an array of lower-intensity lamps would achieve the same result. In this situation, the light was placed a few feet to the left of and just ahead of the camera. Lowering the light would make the effective overhead light source broader, while raising it would produce a punchier image with more contrast range between highlight and shadow.

In figure 7.2, this additional light was positioned at approximately 6 feet high. The reflection off the ceiling, which was about 12 feet high, produced a nice overall fill for most of the objects in the room. The dark walls and gray carpet absorbed the additional shadows produced by the extra light source (it is usually difficult not to have some conflicting shadows in a shot like this since there are about a dozen different lights coming from several directions). Since the added light is being bounced off a white matte surface, no additional diffusion is needed, because it would only diminish the light's intensity. The extra light also did wonders for the ceramic objects by lightening the very dark shadows areas in them so that detail is readable.

Working with Daylight
Avoiding Getting the Blues

Photographing installations that are lit mostly by daylight requires a bit more planning since the natural lighting is constantly varying, both in quantity and quality. Using common sense will help you solve most of the problems this presents. The most important consideration is to determine precisely when the light is best. Unless you are trying to evoke a specific mood, the midday hours usually provide the largest quantity of light and the fewest shadows since the sun is highest in the sky at that time. It is also the time when the glare of the direct sunlight is usually on the floor rather than on the walls. It is often best to have *indirect* natural light shine on the

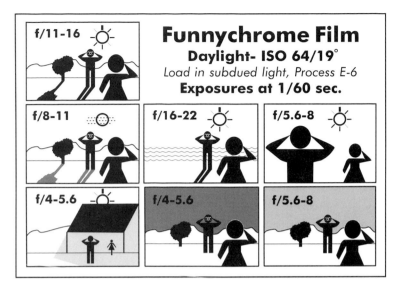

Figure 7.3. A film data sheet as supplied by manufacturers. Many art objects look best when photographed in open shade because it generally ensures adequate shadow detail. If left unfiltered in open shade, many E-6 films produce a bluish cast caused by the reflection of the sky onto the object.

objects because the quality of indirect light is less intense and more evenly spread. Less work and little to no additional lighting or reflectors are required to make quality photos when the natural light is indirect. You also avoid the problems of hot spots and outlines of window frames created when the light is shining directly on the walls. (This is the reason many painters like to work with a cool, indirect Northern light in their studios.)

Unless the floors and walls are warm colors, the color temperature of most indirect light is on the cool side. Have a few of the warming filters on hand, such as the ones described in the previous section, especially if you are using a higher speed E-6 film made in the United States or Europe. These films will produce a readily apparent bluish cast if unfiltered, so start your test with an 81C and adjust from there. Warming filters are also good for "open shade" shooting situations outdoors.

Open shade (see the film exposure sheet in figure 7.3) is the most natural form of indirect lighting. The sun is blocked by some object, such as a tree or a building, and the only illumination is the indirect light of the rest of the sky. If the sky is blue, then the indirect light is blue as well. The photographic results on transparency film will be blue, too, if you don't add the necessary filtration (when shooting color negative film, this filtration is usually added during the printing process).

All the rules that apply to photographing three-dimensional objects inside should be used outside. You should use fill reflectors to increase shadow detail whenever possible. For very large objects, like building exteriors or outside frescoes that are hard to light or reinforce artificially, it is necessary to do a bit of research to discover the optimum time of day and weather conditions for the best photo. Take a camera with you and shoot a few frames during each visit, keeping a very detailed record of the time and weather. If these shots don't work, try to anticipate what would improve them (lower or higher sun, more or less diffusion) and reshoot when the conditions are more optimal.

Generally speaking, most objects will look best when photographed midmorning or midafternoon. I also like days when there is a thin, high overcast that diffuses the light somewhat but doesn't eliminate shadows altogether. This is the light I most often re-create in the studio.

Most outside installations are carefully planned and executed by the artist, architect, owner, or curator to achieve a certain effect, which by necessity includes the environmental lighting. Placement and direction will determine the optimum time for photography. If you created the object and installed it, you should already know under what conditions it will look best. If you were not part of the planning, talking to the people who were should provide you with a starting point. If the installation is well planned, the best photography approach should be self-evident.

But often the planners had to make compromises, or simply did a bad job. Or a new building is erected that blocks the intended natural lighting. Whenever something like this occurs, you need to observe and improvise.

If you are not pleased with midmorning or midafternoon light, try early-morning or late-afternoon light. The light quality may be very warm the hour after sunrise and the hour before sunset, calling for some blue filtration.

Some objects look best when photographed on one of those thick, overcast days with a "concrete" sky. This is especially true for objects with strong, deep colors. The heavy overcast lowers the image contrast and allows the colors to become completely saturated and luminous (see figure 7.4).

You can get a very interesting effect by shooting after a rainfall, when the sun is just beginning to shine. The wetness sometimes adds richness to the environment's colors. The rain also masks many imperfections (bad pavement, faded

7.4. A recent rain and heavy overcast skies helped to accentuate the bright colors in this outdoor sculpture by Viola Frey. The rain also made the grass and trees more vivid and fresh, enhancing the overall background for the photograph.

paint, uneven lawns, dirty windows, etc.). The addition of water to normally dry elements in the environment, for example concrete pavement, will deepen and even out their overall shade while creating highlights wherever there is the least amount of standing water. On the object itself, wetting the surface can minimize accumulated dirt or dust. It can also make many matte surfaces look glossier. If the weather is uncooperative, it may be worth the trouble and effort to hose down the installation and create this effect.

All in all, don't be discouraged if you don't get the shot you want the first time out. My experience at most location shoots when I have been dependent on using natural light is that I often need to go back two or three times before I am content with the photographic result. Getting the perfect shot is a matter of patience and timing. Time constraints may make it necessary to photograph in less than perfect conditions, but with persistence you will get the shot you want.

8

Using a 4 × 5 Camera

When Bigger Is Better

Compared to 35mm cameras, a 4 × 5-inch view camera is much simpler mechanically. Its origins go back thousands of years to the *camera obscura* (Latin for "darkened room"), first described in detail by Aristotle. He observed the projected images of solar eclipses on the ground made through the very small holes of a sieve. The smaller the hole was, the sharper the image became.

Over the centuries this idea was refined into a widely used scientific and artistic tool. Glass optics replaced the pinholes, but the principle was the same—light was projected through a small aperture onto a surface in a darkened room so that it could be easily observed and traced by hand. By the sixteenth century, artists could use different focal length lenses, as we do today, to change the perspective or to make detailed and accurate portraits and architectural renderings.

The problem was that these darkened rooms were fixed structures in existing buildings and allowed only limited points of view. In the early seventeenth century, a portable camera obscura, the size of an average room, was created to record nature and architecture on site; it required today's equivalent of a moving van to move the camera. By the end of that century the camera obscura, although still large and bulky, evolved into a form remarkably similar to the 4 × 5 view cameras we use today. "Permanent" photographic images became possible in the mid-nineteenth century, and photographers were able to record any type of subject matter with relative ease.

Many people find today's 4 × 5 view cameras bulky and clumsy to use when compared to the miniature 35mm. However, the reward for the extra effort is an image area (20 square inches) that is over thirteen times larger than a 35mm image (1.5 square inches).

A high-quality 4 × 5 will always be better than a 35mm image for reproduction, since it doesn't need as much enlargement. Also, a 4 × 5 transparency is large enough to permit viewing of fine detail without projection, making it easier for gallery owners and museums to scrutinize your work. And, it makes a much more impressive presentation.

One drawback is that the film and processing will cost generally more than eight times the amount of that of 35mm cameras. Most artists I work with become a bit more selective in the artwork they photograph with a 4 × 5 to keep costs from skyrocketing beyond their budget.

The Equipment
Meeting New Standards

View cameras come in various sizes: 2½ × 3¼ inches, 4 × 5 inches, 5 × 7 inches, 8 × 10 inches, and 11 × 14 inches. The 4 × 5 is a good choice for photography of art because of its moderate acquisition and operating costs when compared with the others (see figures 8.1 and 8.2). It is also the most popular view camera format, so film, accessories and lenses are readily available. Even the least expensive 4 × 5 cameras will produce image quality considerably better than any 35mm camera. Compared to the familiar 35mm camera, any view camera appears huge and looks rather primitive, especially the ones made of wood. But in fact, the typical design of most view cameras offers greater flexibility and finer image control than any 35mm.

The primary advantage is that most view cameras allow you to adjust the relationship of the lens to the film plane, in all

Figure 8.1. A 4 × 5 optical bench monorail view camera.

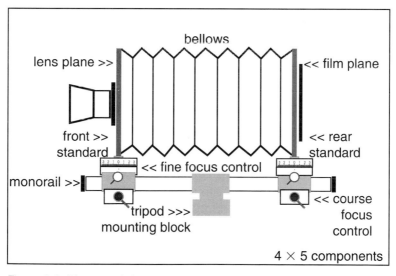

Figure 8.2. Diagram of view camera components.

Figure 8.3A. The camera movement's front standard rise.

Figure 8.3C. The camera movement's front and rear standard swing. Note the relationship to the monorail.

Figure 8.3B. The camera movement's front standard tilt.

directions and on all axes (see figures 8.3A–C). The example shown is a monorail type, most widely used in studios. Field cameras (see figure 8.4) fold compactly for transport but don't have as many convenient adjustments. Both types cost about the same, so the added flexibility and ease of use make the monorail type a better choice for photographing artwork indoors.

On the other hand, a 35mm camera has only one adjustment—the focus—that changes the physical distance of the lens elements to the film. Focusing a view camera is very different indeed, since most allow you to move the film plane (on the back standard) and the lens (on the front standard) independently on the monorail or flatbed. There is a very simple rule to follow that will make operation easy to understand:

The *front standard* (lens) is moved to change *image* size.
The *rear standard* (film plane) is moved to change *focus*.

This allows the user to make small and precise adjustments of image size without moving the tripod and camera. To increase image size, move the front standard toward the subject, then move the rear standard forward until the image is focused. Decreasing image size is just the reverse: move the lens away from the subject, then move the film plane in the same direction to bring the image into focus.

Getting Started
Lens Operation

If you have never used a view camera before, you will first have to know how to look through it! First attach the camera to a tripod extended to about chin level. This should produce a comfortable standing position while you look through the camera. Adjust it as necessary and make sure that every tripod adjustment is adequately tightened.

Next, go to the lens end of the camera and make sure that the lens caps are off. There may be one on both the front and back. Refer to the instruction manual for lens board removal if you need to get to the back cap.

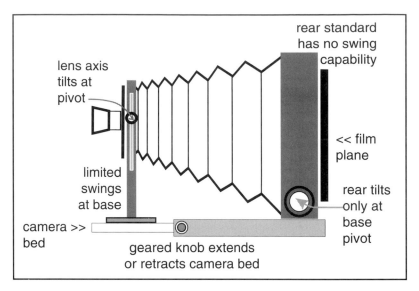

Figure 8.4A. A field camera.

Figure 8.4B. A field camera folded up.

Once the caps are off, find the aperture numbers (refer back to figure 8.3C) to see if the indicator is at the maximum f-stop (the smallest number). If it isn't, follow the trail of the f-stop pointer to a knob that will allow you to change the aperture setting to maximum. Sometimes this knob is just below the pointer; often it is offset considerably to allow for easier viewing of the setting.

Most modern shutters have a preview knob (to the right of the aperture index in figure 8.6) that opens and closes the shutter, which is usually built into the lens; find this knob and push it back and forth to determine the open position. If you see the aperture blades at all, recheck the aperture setting to make sure it's at the maximum f-stop. Anything less than maximum will make viewing dimmer.

Focal Lengths for View Cameras
What the Bigger Numbers Mean

Note the focal length indicated on the lens, usually marked on the front barrel in millimeters. If it says 240mm, then you have a slightly longer than normal focal length lens (161mm is normal, see figure 8.5 for comparisons with 35mm lenses) for a 4 × 5 format. For the metrically impaired, 240mm is about 10 inches; there are approximately 24mm to the inch. The focal length is an important number to remember since it will be the distance between the lens and the film plane for the camera when focused at infinity (the shortest distance between the film plane and the optical center of the lens that will produce a sharp image on film, and the first point when all objects at extreme distance are in sharp focus). To be focused on anything closer, let's say 10 feet, the film plane would have to be moved farther away from the lens. For right now, move both standards equally from the center until they are 10 inches apart so that the lens is approximately focused at infinity, and point the lens at a distant object.

The black cloth packed with the view camera, or purchased separately, is used as a focusing aid. With your head 6 inches directly behind the ground glass, place the dark cloth over your head and the rear standard, wrapping it as much as necessary to

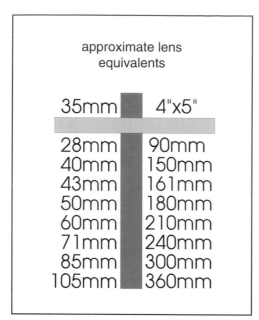

Figure 8.5. 35mm to 4 × 5 lens conversion chart.

block out extraneous light. If everything has been done just right, you'll see the largest camera image you ever saw. If the image doesn't look sharp, loosen the locking mechanism on the back standard and move it until the image snaps into focus.

More About Focusing
Fixated on Sharpness

Extremely accurate focus is achieved by using a *lupe* (an optical device that magnifies a section of the image when placed on the ground glass). Photographers call this process *critical focusing*. Even the inexpensive plastic lupes do an adequate job, so there is no reason to be without this essential tool. The idea is to bring the image into coarse focus by viewing the whole screen, then to make the critical final adjustments aided by the lupe.

Many view cameras, like the one in figure 8.6, have two separate focusing controls. The coarse adjustment knob moves the whole standard along the monorail while the fine focusing

Figure 8.6. Micrometer drive. The outer knob controls the drive, the inner knob locks it into position. The coarse focusing mechanism moves the whole mounting block just below the micrometer drives. Its locking mechanism is out of view on the far side.

knob drives a micrometerlike gear for very small changes in focus. These micro-drives are very handy and necessary when photographing any objects close-up, such as jewelry, where small camera movements create large image differences. Once you use a camera with a full range of micro-drives, you'll wonder how photographers ever got along without them.

The View in a View Camera
What You See Is What You Get?

Looking through a view camera can be disorientating in the beginning because the image is not only upside-down but also laterally reversed (see figure 8.7). Left is right and right is left. The image is also considerably darker because the lens has a much smaller aperture (f 5.6 to f 9.0 are typical) compared to lenses for your 35mm SLR. The novice's initial reactions range from the amused to the truly frustrated.

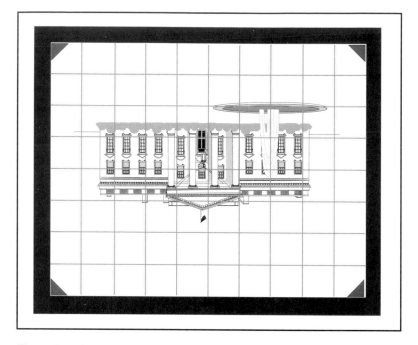

Figure 8.7. An image as seen through a view camera. The larger viewing area makes initial orientation and adjustment easier than expected.

Your 35mm SLR has a prism that flops the image about so that it appears "correct"; such a prism for a 4 × 5 would be incredibly heavy, bulky, and prohibitively expensive. However, working with a 4 × 5 gets easier with a little experience. View camera users quickly learn to read upside down.

Camera Movements and Lens Coverage
A Shifting Point of View

As mentioned before, modern view cameras have many additional image adjustments, called *movements*, not available to 35mm users. Each movement has a logical name. Moving the lens or film plane left or right is called a *shift* (see figure 8.8). Moving the lens or film plane up is called a *rise*, while moving them down is called a *fall* (see figure 8.9). These are extremely

Figure 8.8. Top view of a 4 × 5 camera showing a front standard shift to the right. Note the standard's relationship to the monorail.

Figure 8.9. The camera movement's rear standard rise.

useful features for any view camera work. The amount of movement available will be determined by the design limits of the camera, the attached lens focal length, and lens type (wide-angle, normal, or telephoto).

Lens manufacturers often produce several versions of lenses for any given focal length, each with a specific application. A 210mm lens of general-purpose design will typically cover a 70-degree angle of view, producing a circular image 295mm wide (about 12 inches) when focused *at infinity* (minimum distance between the lens and film plane). The image circle gets progressively larger the closer the focus (see figure 8.10). The equivalent lens in 35mm only covers 46 degrees, creating an image circle just large enough to cover the 35mm film. The extra 24 degrees designed into the view camera lens allows the 4 × 5-inch film to be moved several inches in each direction using the camera's adjustments.

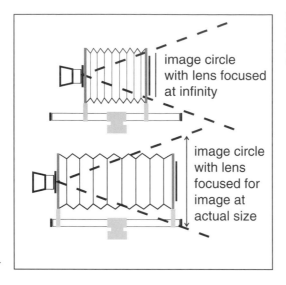

Figure 8.10. The relationship between reproduction ratio and image circle size.

The 105-degree lens produces an image circle 365mm wide focused at infinity, large enough for full coverage using an 8 × 10-inch camera, and is designed as a wide-angle lens for that format. It is also incredibly expensive and not really practical for 4 × 5 use. The most common 4 × 5 wide-angle lens has a 90mm focal length.

A few specialty 210mm lenses have only a 48-degree coverage and would allow for seemingly limited camera movements since the image circle (180mm) would be just larger than 4 × 5 inches when focused at infinity. However, most of these lenses are optimized for close-ups, when the lens must be farther from the film plane and will naturally produce a larger image circle.

Choosing the Right Lens
The Optimal Optical

The 210mm focal length with 70-degree coverage is a good choice for photographing art. It is slightly longer than a "normal" lens, which is 161mm, and produces a flatter yet pleasing perspective about halfway between a normal and a "portrait" lens (322mm). Most lenses in the 300mm range are made for

Figure 8.11. This 4 × 5 view camera has a maximum bellows extension of 500mm. This allows a 1-to-1 image with lenses up to 250mm focal length. It would allow a 2-to-1 image magnification using a 125mm lens.

8 × 10-inch cameras and are considerably more expensive, but their coverage far exceeds the movement capability of any 4 × 5.

The 210mm is the most popular product photography lens. The 210mm is a bit more costly than slightly shorter focal lengths (180mm or 150mm), but not excessively. The price difference is easily offset by the lens' increased capabilities and overall usefulness.

Although new lenses are always nice to own, any good lens design from the last thirty years will suffice for even the most critical work. If you are in the market for a used lens, the larger cities usually offer more selection; mail-order stores can be convenient for the truly rural. Just make sure they have a money-back guarantee in case you are not satisfied with the results.

If you are doing close-up work, you must match the focal length carefully with the total amount of bellows extension permissible with your 4 × 5. To photograph an object at exactly life-size on film, the distance from the lens to the film plane will be exactly double the focal length. If you are using a 210mm lens, you must be able to extend the bellows 420mm to shoot something life-size. Some models are incapable of this much extension, so a shorter focal length lens, like 180mm or 150mm, would have to be used to insure that capability.

The camera in figure 8.1 has a bellows extension of 500mm, allowing use of up to a 250mm lens to still shoot life-size on film. Many specialized close-up lenses, usually referred to as apochromatic or "apo" lenses, are available only in slightly longer focal lengths of 210mm, 240mm, 250mm, and longer. These lenses are optically designed to work best within a very specific reproduction size. For example, several of my lenses are their sharpest when the image is one-tenth to three-quarters life-size on film. Just outside the optimum reproduction range, these lenses yield perfectly usable images. If the range is greatly exceeded, especially larger than life-size, image quality rapidly diminishes.

Apochromatic lenses are made with very special and expensive optical glass so that they focus the entire spectrum of light onto virtually the same plane. This is very important for close-up lenses because the image and any optical irregularity is often greatly magnified.

General-purpose lenses are designed for use at much lower magnifications and wouldn't benefit from the extra quality control and expensive optics needed to make apochromatic lenses. If you use a general-purpose lens for extreme close-ups, you may get very small but noticeable halos of color around the edges of the object in the photo. Many other factors will determine just how noticeable these halos will be. Using apo lenses produce images with none of these defects.

Apo lenses are wonderful for all studio applications and critical color photography. Most of the time, they are essential for photographing small objects, like jewelry. Unfortunately, these lenses are more expensive and usually have a maximum aperture of f9.

Sheet Film and Film Holders

The simplest, most cost effective way to package film and load it into a view camera is to use precut film sheets. These

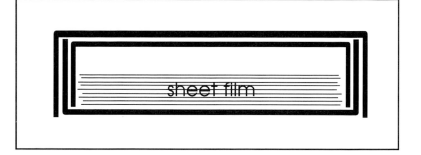

Figure 8.12A. Side-view diagram of a sheet film box. The three component boxes form an effective light trap in most situations. It is prudent to avoid placing boxed live film on strong light sources such as light boxes or tables.

Figure 8.12B. The top two parts of the film box would normally be inverted and inserted into the bottom part to form the light trap. Secure the boxes with tape or elastics to prevent accidental opening.

sheets are considerably thicker than film spooled on 35mm rolls. Manufacturers box sheet film in lots of 10, 25, 50, and 100. The construction of the box itself is very ingenious—it has an additional cover that creates an extremely effective light trap (see figures 8.12A and B) so that any film inside can be safely protected from external light penetration.

On the short side of the film are identification notches that allow you to identify the type of film by feel in the dark (figure 8.13). Somewhere on the outside of each box of film, and on the data sheet packed inside, is an illustration of the film's

Figure 8.13. Sheet film has identification notches along one short side of the film. The notches also help you properly orient the emulsion. In this example, the emulsion is on the reverse side.

identification notches. These notches also help identify the emulsion side that must be facing the lens inside the camera.

The film sheet is loaded emulsion-side up inside a two-sided holder (see figure 8.14). Two small rails hold the film flat while a dark slide keeps it from being exposed when not inserted in the camera. The dark slide is inserted with its indicator showing white or silver for unexposed film, or is flipped over showing black for film already exposed.

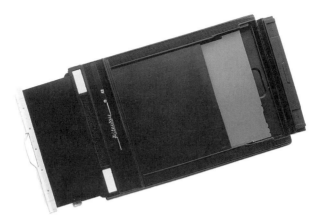

Figure 8.14A. A 4 × 5 sheet-film holder with the dark slide partially removed and the end flap open.

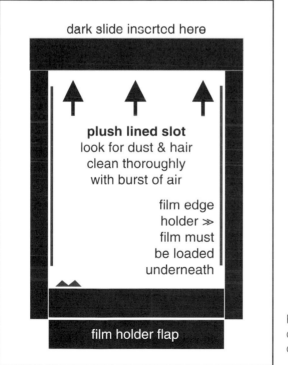

dark slide inserted here

plush lined slot
look for dust & hair
clean thoroughly
with burst of air

film edge
holder ≫
film must
be loaded
underneath

film holder flap

Figure 8.14B. Diagram of sheet-film holder components.

Loading Sheet Film
Stacking the Case for Darkness

Almost all sheet film must be handled and loaded in complete darkness. Most photographers can conveniently use their printing darkrooms for this purpose, but even here some additional care must be taken with keeping external light out. Film is extremely light sensitive, much more than black-and-white printing paper. A darkroom can be full of light leaks that will have no adverse effects on a photographic print, but even the smallest amount of external light could spell disaster for film. If you plan to use a darkroom to load film, follow these procedures beforehand:

1. Take a few old towels, some black construction paper, scissors, and black tape into the darkroom. Roll the towel up and placed it on the floor behind the door after it is closed; push the towel with your foot until the whole width is covered. This gap is usually the biggest source of unwanted light in any darkroom.

2. Make covers with the construction paper for everything that is luminescent, such as darkroom timers. Use the tape as a hinge so that the cover can be flipped out of the way when not in use. It might have been safe to have timer lights exposed for a few minutes when you developed paper prints, but it's unsafe for the fifteen to thirty minutes it takes to load or unload thirty sheets of film. Also cover any type of electronic equipment, such as a stereo, that have backlit dials and bright indicator lights. A cover may do the trick, but directly taping each light source with thick black tape is far more effective.

3. At the brightest part of the day, or with every external light outside the darkroom switched on, go into the darkroom and turn off all the lights and wait ten to twenty minutes for your eyes adjust to the darkness. Try not to expose your eyes to bright light, even momentar-

ily, for one hour prior to entering the darkroom. This will help preserve your "night vision" or light sensitivity to help find and block out even the faintest amount of light. Use the black tape and construction paper to cover any leaks while you are still in the dark. When you are certain that there are no more leaks, turn on the light and secure the paper and tape permanently. Turn out the lights once more and repeat the test. Your darkroom is now ready for sheet film work.

Other Options
Taking Over the Closet

Closets also make excellent film loading rooms, as long as you have enough space to stand up and an 8 × 18-inch shelf for a work area. For years, I used a fold-down shelf in one of my storage rooms to load sheet film. This allowed me to simultaneously operate my wet darkroom and to store my film away from chemicals and liquids. Follow all of the preceding recommendations to secure a closet from light.

Changing bags are another option. They are really double-layer bags that have tight-fitting sleeves that allow your hands access to the inner light-tight compartment. Changing bags fold very compactly and can easily fit into a camera case, making them very practical for location work. If you go this route, make sure that the bag is large enough to handle a dozen holders and a few boxes of film. Always keep these bags free from dust that can easily fall on your film while loading.

Portable changing rooms are similar to changing bags except that they are held open by a frame that can fold compactly for storage. In these rooms you can move your hands more freely and also keep the inner liner from coming in close contact with or touching the film or the holder's surface, as it always does in a changing bag. You will also eliminate most of the dust problem with any reasonable amount of caution. The changing room is about three times more expensive than a bag.

Preparing the Holders
Recipe for Success

Once you have selected and have available a proper loading area, the next step is to prepare the holder for loading. On a clean, dust-free surface, stack all the holders into one pile to your left. Take the top holder and pull the dark slide completely out. Using a can of compressed air or a large ear syringe, blow all the dust out of the holder and off its surface, including the hinged flap at the end. Also make sure that the black plush padding (used to trap light when the dark slide is removed, see figure 8.14B) is dust and hair free. Clean both sides of the dark slide and insert it halfway with the white indicator exposed. This is the marking for unexposed film. Flip over and repeat.

As each holder is cleaned, stack it in a pile to the right. With the dark slide handle facing you, take the cleaned stack of holders and move them again to your left if you are in a dark room, or insert them into the changing bag or room, but again to the left. Place the film box to the right of the holders, turn out the lights, and zip the bag shut. If you are in a room, give a quick check to make sure the door is securely shut and there are no obvious light leaks before opening the film box.

Boxing Procedures
Striking Out in the Dark

Open the first (and largest) layer of the film box and flip it onto the back of the next largest layer. Take the inner layer and flip it 180 degrees, so that all three layers are facing the same direction. The film itself is packaged between two pieces of cardboard in a sealed envelope. Tear one end of the envelope, remove, and discard it. Find the film notches and place the film back in the box with the notches positioned to the upper right.

Pick up a holder in your left hand and flip open the flap (the dark slide was only halfway inserted when the holder was cleaned). With your right hand, pick up a piece of film by the edges of the notched area and insert fully under the rails in the film holder. It's easy to miss the rails, especially at first. You can test that the film is properly loaded by giving the film a little upward tug. There is a little divit in the film holder next to the film notches to assist in this. The end should flex up just a little, but the film won't move. If it moves or pops out, pull the whole sheet out and start again.

Make sure that the emulsion side is up by checking that the film notches are in the right corner at the flap end (see figure 8.14B). You can use the notches later to check your film type if you forget what type is in the holder. With the film properly placed, push the dark slide in fully. If you can't push it all the way in or if you feel the film bending, pull the slide part of the way out again and make sure that the film is inserted fully. Recheck and push the slide closed.

Flip the holder over and repeat. When both sides of the holder are loaded, place the holder to the right of the box. Continue until all the holders are loaded and stacked to the right. Close the box correctly to maintain the double light trap, and secure with a rubber band to prevent accidental opening. You can now safely turn on the lights.

You may want to practice all the above in light first with a processed or scrap sheet film. Move on to practice in the dark (or in a changing bag) until confident. It is very important to learn how to handle the film by the edges without touching the image area. Natural oils or moisture on your fingers can leave permanent, FBI-quality fingerprints on any part of the film that is touched. Wash and dry your hands before loading or unloading film. Changing rooms and bags are efficient heat traps; whenever your hands start to perspire, close the film box and pull your hands out to dry.

Shooting Flat Artwork with the View Camera

View camera setup for flat art is easier than the setup for a 35mm. There is one and *only* one perfect 35mm camera placement that will reproduce the flat art in natural perspective; but view cameras only need to be placed in an approximate

Figure 8.15. Spirit levels on the camera's rear standard. This arrangement has one bubble level for the vertical (film) axis and another for longitudinal axis. Some cameras have only one level where you center the bubble into a circle.

position. You can use the camera's versatile movements to correct imperfect angles and perspectives.

For paintings hung on walls, it is best to start the setup with all the camera movements centered and the tripod legs extended to bring the lens height to just below the center (top to bottom). This allows you to alter the height of the tripod's center column for final, easy adjustment, rather than adjust the tripod's legs, which is a difficult task because of by the camera's weight. A geared center column makes it even easier.

Next, find the built-in level (see figure 8.15) and adjust the tripod head to enter the bubble indicators. Most cameras have two sets of levels, one on the front standard and another on the rear. If one set is level and the other isn't, one of the movements, usually the tilt, is off. When all levels are centered, the camera should be square with the walls.

Set the camera up on the line extending perpendicularly from the center eft to right) of the flat art and move the camera closer or farther away or out until the image almost fills the ground glass. Leave at least a 1/4-inch border on all sides. This border comes in handy when you put a presentation matte on the transparency. Also use the border when you are holding or hanging the film to keep the image area clean of fingerprints or processing hanger marks.

The ground glass of almost all view cameras can be positioned for a vertical or horizontal shot by removing and reattaching the film back appropriately (see your camera's user's manual). Some have a rotating back that can be positioned and locked at any angle, with positive indents to identify the 90 and 180 degree angles. Choose the appropriate vertical or horizontal format for your camera.

"Squaring" the Image
Getting the Right Angles

If the artwork is square or rectangular, use the etched grid markings on the ground glass to square the camera to the art. The "squaring" process is greatly simplified if the artwork is carefully leveled and flush with the wall. When that is done, loosen the tripod head so that you can pan it very short distances side to side. When the top and bottom are parallel with the horizontal lines of the focusing screen grid, lock it in place. You may want to raise or lower the back standard to place one of the grid lines on or just outside the edge of the art. This will allow you to see even the slightest amount of skew or image distortion.

Adjust the shift on the back standard to center the image left to right, if needed. If the sides of the artwork are parallel with the vertical grid lines, the image is now distortion-free. However, if both sides of the artwork slant to the center at the top, even just a little, the camera is pointed up at the art and therefore not parallel to it. Use the tripod head to lower the lens until the sides are parallel (check critically with a four to ten power lupe). This will shift the image down on the focusing screen, leaving a larger border at the top of the screen (which is actually the bottom part of the artwork since you are viewing the image upside down). Center the image by raising the front standard.

If the sides of the artwork appear slanted in at the bottom, the camera is pointed downward at the art. Correct this distortion by tilting the camera up and center the image by raising the back standard.

The real problem comes when three sides are square but the fourth is askew. If you have a builder's square handy, go up and put it on each corner of the artwork. What may look square to the eye can be pretty far out of whack when put to this test. If the corners measure up, see if the frame is completely flat against the wall. Warped frames are very common and should be expected.

If the artwork measures square but only one side is "off" in the image, the camera is off center axis both vertically and laterally (left and right). Redo the appropriate steps until the image appears correct.

If the artwork does not have perfect right angles, or if your image is still not square after these first adjustments, there are a few more controls, the swings and tilts of the *rear* standard, to try (we are assuming that the front standard is perfectly parallel with the art, as it should be). It may take a combination of both tilt and swing (less than 10 degrees each) to accomplish a better rendition. Unfortunately, each movement will affect the other. Be patient and observe the effects of each on the image. If the image gets too off line, just center the movements and start again. Though the final image may not be perfectly correct, it is better than proceeding with no corrections at all.

The preceding may sound complicated, but in practice it's very simple and generally quicker than setting up a 35mm. The additional controls and the large 4×5 image allow a precision unavailable to small cameras.

Film-Shooting Procedures for the 4×5
The 1, 2, 3s for Your 4×5

A number of steps are necessary to expose film in a view camera since virtually no controls are automated, as is commonplace with 35mm cameras. First, insert the film holder into the camera by pulling at the opening at the shorter side of the ground glass. Push the holder in fully and close the back. Many brands have a spring-loaded lever to assist in smooth operation (see you camera's user's manual). Inspect the camera back to make sure it is completely closed and the film holder is fully inserted. Also check the indicator strip (white or silver) on the dark slide to verify that the film on that side of the holder is unexposed.

Then go look through the lens. Move the preview lever to the closed position and check that the shutter blades close completely. Next, set the appropriate aperture, and then the shutter speed. Most lenses are optimized in the f22–f45 range, although f16 could be used in a pinch. There are many tungsten sheet films on the market that permit long exposure times of up to thirty seconds. These films allow you to use the small but typical view camera apertures with even low-powered lights. Use the B or T setting and a watch with a second hand for timing.

Cock the shutter and test fire it with the cable release. Most shutters will not fire if the preview lever is in the open position, even partially. If the shutter does not fire, recheck all settings and try recocking the shutter. Repeat until you hear or see the shutter cycle. If you are using the T setting, you must push the cable release twice. The first opens the shutter, and the second closes it. The B setting is similar, except that the down stroke opens the shutter and keeps it open until the pressure is released. Do not continue until you hear or see these two actions using the B or T shutter setting.

Then recock the shutter, pull the dark slide out completely, and fire the shutter. The film is now exposed. Flip the dark slide so that the black indicator is facing out and insert fully back into the film holder. Open the camera back and remove.

If you are shooting duplicate or bracket exposures of the same object in succession, it is not necessary to test the shutter each time. Simply insert a holder with unexposed film, cock the shutter, check or adjust the aperture, pull the dark slide, shoot, insert dark slide, and repeat. Keeping exposed film holders in a separate stack will help avoid mistakes. I keep unexposed film holders close to the camera and exposed film holders at least a few steps away as a farther hindrance to accidentally confusing one for the other.

You may want to practice all these procedures several times before exposing real film, especially since each sheet of color film will cost $4 to $5 with processing. At this point, continue by following the final shooting checklist for flat art on page 51. Also be sure to read the Polaroid section at the end of this chapter, page 196.

Shooting Three-Dimensional Artwork with the View Camera

I am often required to shoot both 4 × 5 and 35mm film of the same object. But I always start with the 4 × 5 since there are several advantages view camera users enjoy over 35mm when shooting three-dimensional work. The most obvious advantage is that the much larger working image makes it possible to see details and subtleties clearly. Lupes placed directly onto the ground glass further enhance this advantage.

The larger image size also aids precision in composition. The camera movements allow easy and minute adjustments for framing. And using a Polaroid film holder lets me test the lighting and exposure, seeing the results in less than a minute. Once you are familiar with your view camera and accustomed to its advantages, you may not want to use anything else.

Getting Started

With all camera movements centered and locked, set up your first shot as you would with any camera. Next, choose either a vertical or horizontal format and allow a certain amount of space around the object so that it doesn't look cramped within the picture frame. Use the shifts and rises to make small final image positioning adjustments. If large adjustments are required, it's probably best to shift the whole camera.

Many small objects, such as the ceramic pictured in figure 8.16, need no perspective correction at all, even though the camera may be pointed down at a considerable angle. To finish

Figure 8.16. Glazed ceramic by Beatrice Wood, 1987, 18"h. This object will not benefit from camera-movement perspective corrections. In this instance, perspective corrections would require a smaller aperture to insure the same sharpness than if left uncorrected.

shooting preparation be sure to focus with precision. Use a lupe to establish the precise focus point at one-third the distance from the front to the back of the object (see figure 1.3). As long as the reproduction ratio is low (one-sixth life-size or smaller), you can use a small aperture, such as f45, and rest assured that your image will be critically sharp.

Bellows Extension and Close-up Focusing
Bagging the Exposure and Focus Every Time

Larger reproduction ratios, one-sixth life-size and up, require extra exposure and focus consideration. This happens more frequently using a 4 × 5 than with 35mm because you are creating photographic images four times larger initially. If the object is small and has a lot of depth, like the teacup in figure 8.17, focus becomes very critical. If your camera has both coarse and fine-focus adjustments, center the fine-focus indicator and use the coarse control to bring the closest part of the object into sharp focus by looking through a lupe.

Since the image on the ground glass can be very dim, many photographers aim a separate bright light head or spotlight at

Figure 8.17. Ceramic cup by Andrew Lord, 1989, 8"w. When photographed at relatively large reproduction ratios, objects like this cup need to be precisely focused to maximize depth of field. It may be necessary to reduce image size if sharpness cannot be maintained at the smallest useful aperture.

the object when setting the focus. This light is turned off when the focus setting is completed.

Next, use the fine control to focus on the farthest part of the object or background that needs to be sharp. Look at the fine-focus scale (the chrome numbered strip just above the mono-rail in figure 8.16A) and note the indication. This example uses millimeters (each unnumbered little mark and indicates "1" or 10mm). If the scale says the focus has changed 30mm from the front to the back of the object, move the fine focus 10mm back from the starting position, following the depth of field one-third rule (see figure 8.6). This focus setting maximizes the depth-of-field potential.

You still need to select a small enough aperture to ensure that the object's image is crisp and sharp in its entirety. As the lens is stopped down, the zone of sharpness increases in front of and behind the point of focus by a ratio of one to two. The smaller the aperture, the larger the depth of field and the more of the setup that can be in focus. It is not uncommon to use f45 and even smaller apertures for three-dimensional work.

The preview knob will open the shutter so that you can check the image sharpness at the intended aperture. The image on the ground glass will be very dim at f45. A lupe and an additional focusing light are extremely useful aids in this situation, as would be a Polaroid test shot. If the object does not look sharp throughout at minimum aperture, you will need to move the camera farther from the object to reduce the image size. With view cameras, center the fine-focusing control on the rear standard, then reduce the image size by moving the front standard along the monorail and away from the object. You will need to move the rear standard back, too, until you bring the image into focus. Repeat these steps until you obtain perfect image sharpness throughout.

Also note that when you increase or reduce the reproduction ratio you will need to adjust exposure accordingly. Most 35mm close-up lenses have reproduction indicator readouts. All that you need to do is look up the indicated reproduction size on the chart on page 142, and add the necessary exposure usually given in f-stops.

View cameras have no such indicators, so you need to physically measure how far the bellows (connecting the front and rear standards) is extended to precisely determine how much the light intensity is diminished at that extension. I keep a pocket tape measure in my camera case for this purpose alone.

As mentioned in chapter 6, light intensity decreases proportionally by the square of the distance. For example, if the lens used is 8¼ (210mm) and the measured bellows extension is 16½ inches from lens to the film plane, the light hitting the film is only ¼ the intensity. This is equal to a two f-stop difference, which we then need to add to properly expose the film. This compensation number in f-stops is called the *bellows extension factor*. The example amount of bellows extension also produces a life-size image with a 210mm lens.

Using the same example, if the light meter reads f45 at a given shutter speed, the aperture must be set at f22 to produce the correct exposure. The addition of the bellows extension factor to the actual aperture setting is called the *effective aperture*. In this example, the f22 setting produces an effective aperture of f45 for exposure purposes only. The lens still produces depth of field and sharpness relating to the actual f22 setting.

The example I used was simple since it was based on exactly double the focal length. To determine other settings in between precisely, use the following equation:

$$\frac{\text{the aperture needed}}{\text{focal length of lens}} = \frac{\text{effective aperture}}{\text{bellows extension}}$$

For example, if a 210mm lens was set at f45, and you measured the bellows extension with your metric ruler to be 295mm, the equation would look like:

$$\frac{45}{210} = \frac{X}{295} \quad \text{or} \quad 210X = 13275$$

$$\text{or} \quad X = \frac{13275}{210}$$

$$X = 63.21428571$$

X is the effective aperture, which in this case is very close to f64. Match the shutter speed setting for f64, set the aperture to f45 and shoot.

You can also follow this simple formula:

1. Take the f-stop you want to use and multiply it by the measured bellows length.
2. Divide this sum by the focal length. This is your effective aperture. See figure 8.18B for f-stop scale in one-third stop increments.

Polaroid Film and Holders
Achieving Instant Success

The focusing procedures and exposure techniques mentioned so far all work in theory as long as every piece of equipment functions properly. The best way to catch any error is to take a Polaroid test shot using a 4 × 5 Polaroid back that inserts into the camera just like a film holder.

It's also beneficial to use a Polaroid since lighting and composition are much easier to judge in print form than through a viewfinder. Most problems can readily be identified, corrected, and retested before the shooting the final film (see chapter 10 for troubleshooting).

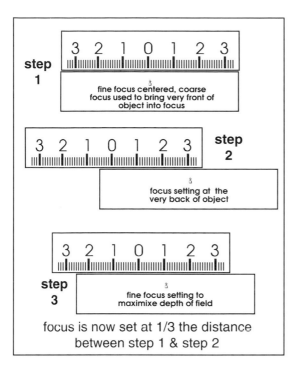

Figure 8.18A. Fine-focusing scale indicators on a 4 x 5 camera. Three-step process for maximizing depth of field when using microdrive indicators.

However, there are some things that Polaroid shots can't help screen, most notably color balance. Color in Polaroids is just too inaccurate to use as a basis for predicting the color in the final photograph. Color accuracy in a Polaroid is a matter of luck. Unless specifically asked to provide color Polaroids, I only shoot black-and-white materials.

Black-and-white is less expensive, more accurate, and consistent in ISO/ASA speed, and provides a reference for photographers shooting with both color and black-and-white film. Some subject or background combinations may not have enough contrast or separation to work as a monochrome. A tan background and a light red object will probably work well in a color shot; in

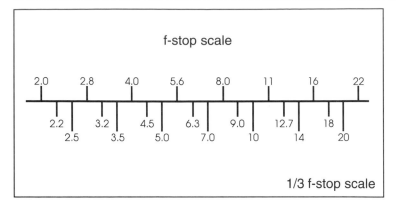

Figure 8.18B. F-stop scale. The top half shows full-stop increments. The bottom half shows the interval 1/3 stops.

black-and-white, however, the values may be so close that it will be impossible to differentiate between the object and the background. But generally, if it works in black-and-white, it will work even better in color.

At this time, there are no general-use *color* Polaroid materials on the market for use when shooting under tungsten lighting. All the color types I've tried have pretty severe reciprocity problems, too. For most photographers, black-and-white may be the only viable choice.

Choose a Polaroid type that has the same film speed as the transparency (or any other) film you intend to shoot. This will help eliminate exposure error caused by the differing film speeds. For example, Polaroid type 54 has a speed of 64 under tungsten light that matches the film speed of several tungsten films. There is nothing to forget or remember when exposing the final film. If the same Polaroid type 54 was used for exposure testing but the film material used for the actual shoot was ISO 125, the lens would have to be set down one additional stop from the aperture used for the Polaroid.

Polaroid 4 × 5 materials come boxed in sealed packages of twenty. Once opened, the remaining film should be protected from moisture with the plastic bag provided. Secure it with a rubberband at one end and store flat in a cool place. I double-bag mine between shoots and put it in the refrigerator to keep it as fresh as possible. *Do not freeze*. This may break the chemical processing pod in each sheet and make a real mess.

Use and Operation
Polaroid Hygiene

All 4 × 5 Polaroid holders have the operating instructions printed right on the holder (see figure 8.19). Read these carefully and check the rollers for cleanliness. If the rollers are dirty, clean them with a cloth, paper towel, or Q-tips soaked in isopropyl (rubbing) alcohol. You are most likely cleaning off processing chemicals that are very potent skin irritants. If you so much as think you have touched these chemicals, be sure to wash thoroughly the affected areas *immediately!*

Dirty rollers produce a number of unpleasant processing defects. If you shoot a lot of Polaroids during a session, flip the cover open and visually check the holder every five to ten shots. It will only take three seconds to do this and may prevent wasting materials.

You also need to read the film instructions packaged in every box. This information sheet tells you how to handle the film and check to see if it is properly loaded. Misloading can cause a real chemical mess, a totally black image, or both. What the info sheet doesn't tell you is that there is usually an audible click when the film is first inserted and the metal strip is hooked to the holder.

If you don't hear that click, the Polaroid holder may be malfunctioning, or the film itself may be defective. The metal strip on one end of the film sleeve is attached to the Polaroid film *negative*, which stays in place when the outer sleeve is pulled out. When this sleeve is pulled out to its fullest extension, the film is ready for exposure. If no click is heard, the film is probably not locked in place and will be pulled out with the film packet's built-in "dark slide." Since the film packet is prevented

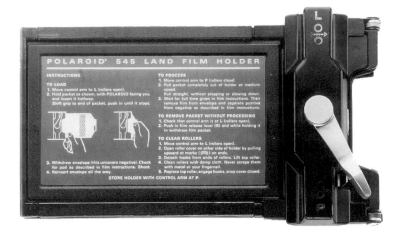

Figure 8.19. Polaroid 4 X 5 film holder. Most have the operating instructions conveniently printed on the back of the holder. Be sure to read the instruction sheet packed with each Polaroid film type.

from coming out whenever the control arm is in the load position, the only way to check for proper loading is by feel (see the film instructions), which is not an easy thing to do.

Most of the time, the trouble is that the Polaroid film packet itself is defective. Occasionally, the rest of the box of Polaroid is defective. To check this, take a shot with a second Polaroid holder to confirm that it's not a malfunction of the first holder. If you get another black image, the problem is more than likely a bad batch of Polaroid film that you had the misfortune to buy. Keep all the bad Polaroids and take the rest of the box back and exchange it for another box with a different batch number.

If the second holder produced a good image, the first holder is probably defective. Try once more with a new film packet and if the result is again black, label that holder defective and tape the slot closed so that it is unusable. Most holders are easily repaired and generally have a long life between failures. Most low-volume, amateur users will never experience a failure. High- volume users own at least two or three Polaroid holders so that they can keep working.

Correcting Perspective
An In-Depth Look

The most common perspective correction, caused by having the camera pointed slightly up or down, is also the easiest to correct. Figure 8.20 shows the effect on a square object. The camera angle causes the sides to be much closer together at the bottom than at the top. This is called *convergence* (to incline together).

Figure 8.21A shows a side view producing an image perspective that is uncorrected. To correct this, the film, lens, and object planes should all be parallel (see figure 8.21B). To get to

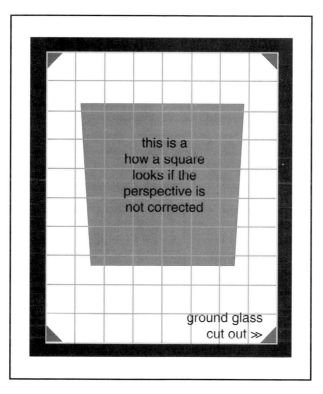

Figure 8.20. The grid lines on the ground glass make it easy to determine and correct image perspective.

this position, center all the movements and frame the object as recommended on page 192 in this chapter. Next, center the bubble in the spirit level by tilting the lens back. Do the same with the back standard. If the supporting table is relatively level, all the objects should look perfectly straight.

If they aren't, determine first if the objects themselves are tilted in one way or another by rotating them while comparing the image to a nearby vertical line on the ground glass. Stop when you find the angle that appears perfectly vertical. If you can't live with the side of the object on view, rotate it 180 degrees and it should also appear perfectly straight up and down. If neither of these faces will do and everything else looks right, wedge paper, cardboard, gum, whatever, under one side of the object until it appears straight. Use a lupe to check the image to make sure the wedge is not visible.

When tilt corrections are made the image will shift a little on the ground glass; use the rise and falls to recenter it. The image of the object will also be slightly larger and must be refocused. If it is now cropped too tightly, reduce the size by moving the front standard back, then refocus with the rear standard. Remeasure the bellows extension, since that also may now be larger, necessitating up to a one-half f-stop exposure increase.

The procedure is the same if you are tilting the camera up, with a few obvious differences; the lens and film planes will be tilted forward.

Lens and Barrel Cutoff
Losing Your Edge

Tilting or swinging the lens excessively (see figure 8.22) will often produce a condition called lens barrel cutoff. This is a form of *vignetting* (fading off to black due to underexposure) caused by part of the lens itself blocking some of the light transmitted through the aperture. A filter or an accessory screwed into the filter ring in front of the lens or the rear lens barrel are the usual culprits. Using one of the smaller apertures, such as f45, will often do the trick.

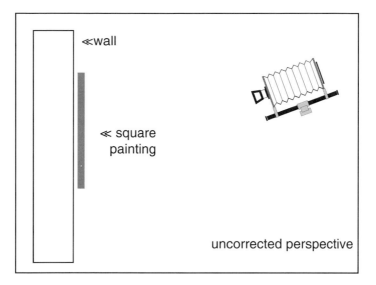

Figure 8.21A. This camera angle will produce the image distortion shown in Figure 8.20.

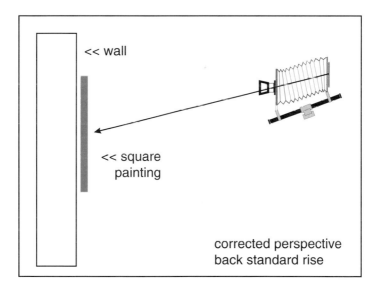

Figure 8.21B. Tilting the front and rear standards to parallel the plane of the art will correct the image distortion produced by the off-axis camera angle.

Figure 8.22A. Front and rear standard tilts may produce vignetting or lens barrel cutoff of the image at the film plane. The lens illustrated is a 70-degree-coverage 240mm. Combined with a bellows draw of about 18 inches (one-half life-size reproduction) the image circle is just large enough to avoid vignetting. A shorter lens, or less bellows draw, would cut off some of the image.

Figure 8.22B. An adjustable lens shade, called a compendium, is a useful accessory that when properly adjusted will allow maximum lens protection from stray light. It is usually adjusted downward, as illustrated, to eliminate flare from an overhead light source placed over a three-dimensional object.

You can use a procedure that ensures the cutoff has been eliminated before you shoot a Polaroid or film. Many manufacturers cut a small diagonal of glass off each corner of the ground glass (see figure 8.23). This allows you to look directly at the rear of the lens through the bellows.

With the shutter open, peer through all four gaps and make sure that all sides of the aperture are clearly visible and look the same. If the view through one gap looks different from the others or is partially blocked, stop down until the aperture blades form a regular, circular pattern. This setting is now the maximum aperture available if you wish to avoid vignetting. You may choose a smaller aperture, but never a larger one. Before

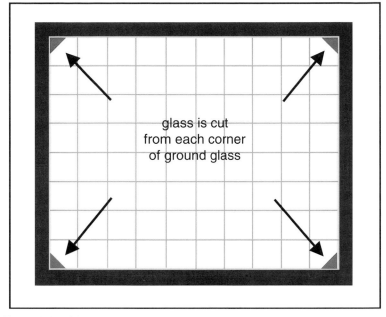

Figure 8.23. Most ground-glass focusing screens have the extreme corners removed. This allows visual confirmation of lens or barrel cutoff.

you shoot, be sure to readjust the shutter to its proper slower speed setting to achieve the right exposure solution.

You will need to readjust the lens tilt if the new slower shutter speed exceeds the film's parameters, or if the cutoff persists even at the smallest aperture. In either case, decrease the camera's swing or tilt until the all of the aperture blades are clearly visible and unobstructed. Remember to retighten the control locks.

Most cameras require readjustment of focus, perspective, image size, and centering after the tilt has been changed. A few very expensive view cameras have sophisticated movement engineering that eliminates all readjustments. However, it only takes a few twist and turns to get everything looking right manually. Just make sure to do it.

Storage and Breakdown

Many photographers put their view camera back into the case only when going to a location site. In most situations, you just need to drape the dark cloth over the camera body if it is to remain on the tripod.

The bellows should be released from any extreme movements or extensions once the shooting session is over. Center all movements and bring the standards close together without completely compressing the pleated folds. This will extend the bellows' life and keep its middle section from sagging prematurely.

View camera lenses all have shutters that should be stored uncocked. Fire the shutter to release the tension; this helps to increase the time between adjustment or repair. Replace both lens caps to protect the delicate lens surfaces from dust and accidental scratches.

If you are putting the camera back into its case, all monorail extensions must be removed, the movements centered, and the rise and fall on each standard lowered all the way down. Remove the camera from its mounting block and compress the bellows just enough to fit it into the center compartment (most cases leave each side compartment for film holders and lenses, respectively).

Some cases require the bellows to be completely compressed in order to fit into its compartment. Any movement that is not perfectly centered will create tremendous stress on the bellows. Always visually check the bellows before storing it out of sight and out of mind.

9

How to Hire a Professional

An Engaging Proposition

No matter how good a photographer you are or want to become, there will be occasions when it will be necessary to hire a professional photographer. Meeting deadlines, having to travel to remote installations, and maintaining your own creative focus head the list of truly credible reasons for hiring a full-time professional to do your photos. Also, you may find that working with a photographer gives you the opportunity to share another's vision about how to interpret your artwork photographically. Oftentimes, a collaboration of this nature can produce stunning results.

And there are just as many, if not more, imaginative and exaggerated *excuses* for just not wanting to do the work. And oftentimes, hiring and watching a pro at work will prove that photographing artwork is not the struggle many artists think it will be. The professional's results can also produce a standard of comparison against which you can measure your own efforts.

The Best Places to Look

The most obvious place to find the right photographer to hire is at your favorite local gallery. If you've done your homework, you already know the quality of the photography from the gallery's announcements, ads, etc. Just look for the photo credit. If there are many different credits, choose the photographer who does the best job on the art that most resembles your own.

In this case, the gallery is already familiar with the photographer's strengths and weaknesses and can make a fairly accurate assessment of your work if they are done by the same photographer. If the gallery can't or won't look at your art physically, photos by their favored photographer is probably the next best thing.

If the gallery photographer isn't suitable, other galleries not specializing in your medium can be good sources of photo talent. Most commercial still-life photographers are great at shooting three-dimensional work. Be prepared to pay healthy fees, though. Still, the benefit is that professionals can meet tight deadlines and produce high-quality reproduction transparencies better and more efficiently than inexperienced amateurs. Always review photographers' portfolios to make sure they can handle your particular art media. Don't ever hesitate to ask a photographer if he or she feels comfortable taking on your assignment.

Most commercial photographers should be able to photograph flat artwork, unless the art is gargantuan in scale. Then, everyone has problems. Photographers who specialize in people most often have trouble doing still-life work. Don't hire portraitists unless they can prove an ability in other areas.

Interviewing the Photographer

Even if you find the absolute best photographer for your work, you still need to show him or her your art and discuss the terms. If the photographer has a studio where the art will be photographed, go there with a representative selection of the work that needs to be documented. If possible, be sure to bring some examples of other photography of your artwork. This provides a useful starting point for discussion that will help the photographer understand your needs.

If he or she is an expert in photographing your medium, the photographer should be able to provide samples of different approaches from which you can choose or modify. Do not let the photographer dominate or dictate the choice—remember it's your art and your dime. The photographer you hire is there to serve your needs. And both parties need to maintain flexibility in arriving at the initial approach. If one photographer seems too rigid, shop around until you find one that is equally talented but relates more to your requests.

I have always produced my best commissioned work when I work closely with the artist through at least a couple of photographs, even with relatively straightforward work such as paintings. I try to find out which colors are important to the artist, those that must be reproduced exactly, because a particular film stock may be needed.

Photographing three-dimensional objects presents a host of options that are often best resolved by looking at samples on the photographic set (these may not be available or not even set up during the initial interview). You must remember that you are getting custom work tailored to your needs and art.

Avoid photo "factories" and catalog houses unless all you need is undemanding copy work. These places usually won't want you there during the shoot, nor will most try anything outside of their basic set of options. It is common knowledge in the advertising industry that such factories usually never do test shots—the first film they shoot is what you get. This is how they keep prices so low. Getting reasonably close is all they can promise. You may get lucky, but don't depend on it.

Seeing Is Believing
Having It Your Way

It may be necessary to leave one or two objects that are truly representative of all the work to be photographed with the photographer. The photographer can make an appropriate lighting setup (mutually agreed upon) and call you when he or she is ready for discussion and approval.

I usually show my clients a 4 × 5 Polaroid at this stage and quite often a film test as well. I may also have set up any other option that seems promising or interesting after working with the object a bit. My client can now easily see which approach works best, or make suggestions that would improve upon this preliminary work.

If nothing looks right, you may have to develop plan B on the spot. The photographer should have alternate plans ready or be prepared to discuss another approach that will work. After all, he or she accepted this work with full knowledge of his or her own limitations and capabilities.

Some art is incredibly difficult to photograph, and more allowances should be given under such circumstance. I always make this perfectly clear to my clients at the outset. It may take several long and tedious efforts to arrive at the right solution. This not only drives up expenses; it drives up the fee the photographer should reasonably expect to charge. Most of the time, I enjoy these challenges, since I usually learn new skills and gain experience.

If you don't get the results you want, shop around and see who else you can find. Professional photographers, like artists, are unique, and are strong in some areas and weak in others. What may take one photographer ten hours to do, another has figured out how to do in one.

For this reason, many pros like to charge on a per-shot basis. With the right experience and skills, some professionals are much more productive than others. Museum curators are amazed how fast shots can be taken by a highly skilled and motivated photographer, as opposed to one who counts the money as the meter runs on a dayrate. Even though a photographer may generate high fees in one day on a per-shot basis, at least you know what the final bill will be ahead of time. When you hire someone on a day rate, you may be in for a shock when presented with the final bill unless you agree beforehand to a specific number of shots to be taken in that day.

In-House Gallery Photographers

Many galleries have a photographer on staff or direct all their photographic work to one or two photographers. For the galleries, there are many benefits to these arrangements: consistency, cost and time savings, and more control over the final product to name a few. Quite often, the image quality is admirable and your work looks splendid. This is quite a bargain for you if the gallery bears all the expense, although this is generally not the case. Most galleries will either split the expense or deduct the full charge from your share of the first sale of one of your pieces. Either of these arrangements may be perfectly acceptable as long as their in-house photographer provides quality work. Problems can arise if the gallery provides you with average- or low-quality photos.

In that case, it is probably best to take control and hire the photographer of your choice, paying him or her directly. This allows you to make the decisions about cost and quality, which is especially important if you have to pay for it all anyway. As long as you deliver as good, or better, photos, your gallery really has nothing to complain about.

If your gallery pays half your out-of-pocket photography expense, they expect to be given a copy of each shot to keep. It's fair for them to pay all the expense of any shot used for advertising since they benefit more than you do from any additional exposure. Try to negotiate this before any work is done. If they do pay half, they should get a say in what kind and how many documentary photos are taken.

Rights and Prices
The Cost of Doing Business

Perhaps the most nebulous, yet vital points in hiring a professional is determining a fair market price for the services. In any given market area, fees and quality may vary considerably. And a high fee may not mean a higher level of quality, although in theory it should. Many factors determine the photographer's pricing structure, notably overhead and a reasonable return of investment for time and money.

As a rule, professionals assess fees according to how the photograph is to be used. Professional organizations publish pricing guidelines for their members. They also publish the circulation figures and ad insertion rates for the top five hundred magazines. The ad insertion rate may be as low as $200 per page to over $100,000 per page every time it is run. For exactly the same shot, the price will vary according to exactly how it will be used.

For example, photo A is used in national consumer ad campaign placed in all the major magazines. The photo fee for that would photo start at $3,000. All things told, the production of that ad could easily run $30,000. If the ad runs five times, the insert could cost a half million dollars. The photography fee may only be one-half of one percent of the total budget.

At the other end of the spectrum is you, the artist. Your work may be photographed just for your own documentation, a grant application, or for your portfolio and may never be published. Rather than try to keep up with how you might use it, most photographers will usually charge you the rate for the lowest tier of media. For this fee, you can reproduce your photo an unlimited number of times inside books (not covers) and inside magazines.

The average published fee (in major metropolitan areas) for this type of use is $75 plus expenses for a straightforward, uncomplicated shot. Some photographers will charge lower, some higher, but it's a fair market price.

For this fee you should get a reproduction-quality 4 × 5 transparency. You and your gallery also have the rights to freely circulate photos of your work for use in articles, books, and show catalogs. Make sure that the photographer gets a credit line any time you reproduce the photo.

But what if you want to sell this same photo to a poster company? Here the law may seem murky to the uninitiated. Unless you specifically obtained all rights from the photographer in writing, you don't have the right to license the photograph or use it for purposes other than those specified in the original agreement. Always make sure to define the reproduction rights to a photo, because even though you may possess a piece of film, the photographer legally owns the image on it.

The publisher is not buying your piece of art—it is buying an image on film, which is the property of the photographer. Rather than run the risk of incurring a legal problem, be sure to inform anyone to whom you give the photo about any reproduction rights or restrictions. It is wise to enclose a delivery memo and have the other party sign both and keep one. The other copy is for your files. Always use a memo when sending your photographs as well. The following is an example of the memo that I use:

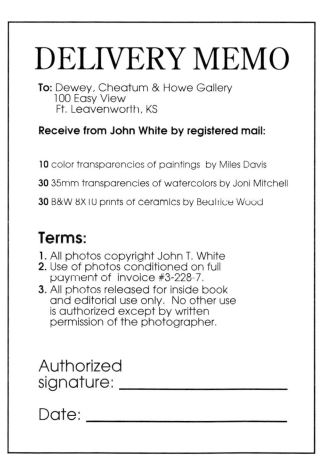

DELIVERY MEMO

To: Dewey, Cheatum & Howe Gallery
100 Easy View
Ft. Leavenworth, KS

Receive from John White by registered mail:

10 color transparencies of paintings by Miles Davis

30 35mm transparencies of watercolors by Joni Mitchell

30 B&W 8X10 prints of ceramics by Beatrice Wood

Terms:

1. All photos copyright John T. White
2. Use of photos conditioned on full payment of invoice #3-228-7.
3. All photos released for inside book and editorial use only. No other use is authorized except by written permission of the photographer.

Authorized
signature: _____

Date: _____

Checklist for Hiring
Professional Photographers

1. Research and ask for recommendations.
2. Interview the photographer and see his or her portfolio to determine if their work is appropriate for your art.
3. Discuss lighting and background options and choose the best one.
4. Ask for a price quote, or settle all fee and rights questions before the shoot starts (this applies to in-house photographers, too).
5. Always use a delivery memo with clearly defined terms.

10

Looking
at
the Results

Love at First Sight?

I always get a great feeling of anticipation when going to the lab to get my test film. It's hard for me to resist pulling the film out immediately and taking a quick look to see if the system still works (and most of the time it does). Over the years, I've become rather skilled at judging my transparencies with just a glance. But to correctly determine whether the exposure, color balance, and composition of your photographs are correct, it is absolutely essential to study them very carefully on a lightbox under controlled lighting.

The importance of your ability to analyze your results and make the necessary corrections cannot be overstressed. Along with basic photography experience, these skills account for the biggest difference between amateurs and professionals. You must also be willing to follow through until you get the very best, truly professional results possible. After a little practice and experience, the color correction concepts in this chapter will become second nature to you.

I've also included a troubleshooting section covering common equipment failures, which are as frustrating to professionals as they are to novices because of the ruined materials, as well as the lost time and effort. Fortunately, most often the problem is easily and inexpensively rectified once you know what to look for.

The Proper Viewing Conditions

Using color correct light boxes is a necessity when you are viewing color transparencies. Even though they are expensive (starting at $300 to $600), they are a lifetime investment for serious photographers. And the only operating cost is bulb replacement. Fortunately, any good-quality lab will have at least one of these light boxes for you to use as part of their customer service. It is ideal when they have one of the high-end models that meter the color temperature and the amount of time the light is on. These types of light boxes enable you to evaluate color that most closely approximates industry standards for reproduction.

Always try to look at your color results on the best box you can find. If your lab doesn't have one or if you are processing through the mail, try photography schools or workshops, rental darkrooms, four-color printers, designers, or architects' offices.

To begin, take out all the slides and lay them out on the light box in numerical order (most labs number them for you—if they don't, ask them to). Place them close together, eliminating the gaps between the slides. Place black construction paper on any uncovered area to block out extraneous light from the box. This bright light makes it harder to judge the *density* (how much light is being transmitted or blocked by the color dyes) of the slide since your eye automatically reacts to the brighter light (in essence it closes the pupil down just like the lens on your camera). Also, turn off all other light sources in the room and draw the curtains to keep your viewing area as consistent as possible.

If the slides are in ascending order, transfer your exposure notes by writing directly onto the cardboard slide mount (with plastic mounts add a small label or use a grease pen). Before looking critically at any one set of exposures, first look at the general density of all your test shots. Are all the images either too light (overexposed) or too dark (underexposed)? If this is the first time you have ever done a test, the answer is often yes. It's time to head back to your test setup and see if there are any obvious mistakes. It's just as easy to make one big mistake as it is three smaller ones, so use the checklist and take another exposure reading, making comparisons at each step. If the transparencies are not even close to being usable images, skip the next section and go directly to exposure and equipment troubleshooting, in the following section.

If you are confident that no mistakes were made, you can continue as long as the results are consistent and *nearly* usable. You will be able to make a one-time correction by calibrating the film speed on your light meter. To do this, you need to refer to your test exposure notes for the middle exposure in the test bracket. If your first results were all too dark (but almost right), you will need to open up one and one half-stops (if your first test used f16 as the middle exposure, use f8$^1/_2$ for the next test). If you first results were all too light, the middle of your bracket will be one and one-half stops down from your original. A new film test is required to verify the new calibration before moving to the next step.

A properly exposed transparency should have readable details in both the highlights and shadow areas of your artwork. If you have one, but not the other, you need to go back and readjust the lighting to lower the lighting ratio (see the chapter covering your particular media). If at least one of the exposures in each bracket looks great, you can move on to the next section and learn how to fine-tune the results. If the middle exposure looks best in most cases, then your camera, meter, film speed is on target.

Exposure Troubleshooting
Nobody Is Perfect

If the best density is consistently the lighter or darker exposure, reshoot any additional transparencies at the correct aperture (leaving the shutter speed constant). The next time you set up to shoot (with the same film, camera, and shutter speed) a simple correction of the film speed on your meter will calibrate the system so that you can hit the mark precisely. Adjust your light meter to a higher film speed if the darker exposure consistently looks best; set a lower film speed if the lightest exposure consistently looks best.

Most meters have films speed indicators that correspond to one-third of a stop, but will usually allow intermediate settings so that a half-stop setting can be set precisely (remember that doubling or halving the film speed is equivalent to an aperture change of one f-stop). If yours does not, first try the one-third stop setting, then the two-thirds stop setting if necessary. Most semiautomatic cameras have a separate ring or knob specifically for film speed or lighting compensations. Check the owner's manual for instructions.

Once you are assured that your complete system is correctly calibrated, you will still have the occasion where the lighter or darker exposure in your bracket looks better as a photograph, even though it is not an exact replica of the artwork. This is very common whenever the art is very light or very dark overall. An example would be a painting made using only black and indigo oils. If the transparency perfectly matched the tones in this painting, little if any surface detail, such as brush strokes, would be discernable. An extra one-half or even one full stop could do wonders for this situation and make it considerably easier for the printer to reproduce the painting accurately.

Camera Settings

If your first test film came back terribly over- or underexposed, begin by rechecking the camera settings. Check the following very carefully:

Exposure meter setting. If you are using ISO 100 film and your meter is set for ISO 400, for example, your photos will be two stops underexposed. Many new cameras automatically set this for you but only work with film that has a bar code and black and silver patches that the meter "reads." If you have this type of camera, make sure that your film has this encoding strip. It has been standard on all film for several years. You might want to check the film's expiration date if your film does not have this coding strip.

Shutter speed and/or f-stop settings. If your shutter is set incorrectly, there will be a one full stop or more error margin. An incorrect f-stop setting will produce at least a half-stop or more error. A half-stop error is not much, but combined with any other error, it can lead to an unusable photograph.

Common Equipment Malfunctions
Helping Your Camera Pass Inspection

If you have double-checked the above and found no errors, the next step is to check each piece of equipment for malfunctions:

Bad battery in camera or meter. Most modern camera batteries work properly until they die and the problem becomes obvious. It is much more difficult to catch a battery that is marginal or isn't working properly because it is being drained or has a bad contact. If the shutter speed is electronically controlled a faulty battery can produce wildly fluctuating results in both metering and exposure. Most cameras and meters have a built-in test mode that will indicate the relative health of your battery. If it tests okay (be sure to check your camera's manual), you can skip to the next step.

If the test is negative or marginal, find the battery compartment and let the battery (or batteries) fall out onto a paper towel or tissue. If you see any leakage or corrosion, don't touch the batteries—just wrap them up and throw them away. Carefully clean out the compartment and contacts and replace with new batteries.

The contacts of both the camera and the battery contact surface should be shiny and clean. If you see any scum or buildup on either surface (caused by moisture or other pollutants in the air) clean each surface (a pencil eraser works well), reinstall, and retest. Many supposedly "dead" batteries are suddenly revitalized this way. If your battery still doesn't test okay (and the camera or meter is obviously not functioning correctly), replace it.

Bad or stuck shutter speed. A partial or total failure of the shutter is easily and readily diagnosed. Remove the lens and open the back of the camera (remove film first). Point the camera toward a constant light source, such as the sky or a well-lit ceiling, and operate the shutter several times at each setting, starting with the slowest speed and continuing to the fastest speed. Each release should be one-half the duration of the previous release; be alert for any irregularities. Carefully observe both the duration and action of the shutter blinds. Did the shutter open at all? Did the speed seem to vary from release to release, even though the shutter setting remained constant? Or did it stay open longer (or shorter) than the set speed? A shutter that is working slower than indicated (causing overexposure) is easier to see and hear than a shutter speed that is too fast (causing underexposure), especially above settings of 1/125th of a second. Specialized equipment is needed to check the accuracy of the fastest speeds, which in general are usually not as accurate as the more often used middle range of shutter speeds. This is especially true in the context of this book, since most of the photography takes place indoors under lower levels of illumination than bright daylight.

A mechanical camera's speeds are often produced by two different gear trains, one for the slower shutter speeds and another for the faster speeds. The shutter may be working perfectly in one gear train and not at all, or badly, in another. This will become obvious as you run up and down the shutter speeds in the test.

If your shutter is electronically controlled the problem is most often a dead battery. A few cameras revert to a single shutter speed (or you can set a manual shutter speed that is predetermined) in the case of a battery failure. A marginal battery may produce wildly fluctuating results, depending on how long the camera has been is on, or on how cold it is. Perform the same shutter speed test and note any discrepancies. Install your spare battery (a good idea for any electronic camera) and repeat the test.

If your problems persist, take your camera to a couple of

local repair shops for estimates for getting it fixed. This is not something that you should try to fix yourself (unless it is just a loose screw on the shutter speed dial). For mechanical cameras, regular maintenance will prevent failures and keep your shutter and built-in meter within operational ranges.

You can also keep track of your camera's health by doing the above tests regularly, or by letting repair shops perform a quick test. I often take my 35mm cameras to manufacturer's clinics that are held in some big cities or at special events. Their technicians are experts on their brand and can identify any problem or answer any question you have in great detail.

Malfunctioning light meter. The light meter is the most delicate part of the camera if it has a needle movement (most newer models have little lights, called LEDs (light emitting diodes), and are much less susceptible to shock). Any good jolt or bounce can hang up the movement permanently, so treat your camera gently. If the battery is good and the meter mechanism is freely moving or lighting up the appropriate lights (see your camera's user's manual) there is a simple and easy test for the general condition of your light meter. For built-in meters set the shutter speed to the same number as the ISO/ASA setting. For example, if the ISO/ASA is set at 64, set the shutter speed to 1/60th (the closest setting to 1/64th); if the ISO/ASA is set at 125, set the shutter speed at 1/125th. Next, point the camera at a clear blue sky away from the sun and take a meter reading The aperture setting should read close to f16 whenever the shutter is set to match the ISO/ASA number. If the reading is more than one full stop off, you have probably found the problem. You may want to do two more tests before you go to a repair shop. Using the same example of ISO/ASA 64, see if the reading remains constant for equivalent exposures (125 at f11, 250 at f8, 500 at f5.6, etc.) and then test the range of ISO/ASA settings.

If all the equivalent exposure settings produce the same reading, you may ignore the meter setting and make your own calibration (if an ASA 64 responds as if it were set to ASA 125 consistently, then set ASA 125 whenever you are using ASA 64 film). Most meters are off a bit and this calibration needs to be done. Most handheld meters allow you to adjust this yourself with the turn of a screw. A repair shop can easily adjust this in your built-in meter, but the cost will range from moderate to expensive depending on the make of the camera. If the meter is functioning perfectly otherwise, you may prefer to make the appropriate notations and adjust your ISO/ASA settings accordingly.

If your built-in meter is producing erratic readings you may try cleaning the contacts again, using another battery (double-check that it is the correct battery or equivalent), and cycling the ISO/ASA setting (if it has one) throughout its range several times and rechecking the results. Many of the film speed dials have electrical contacts within them that may have become dirty, corroded, or stuck. Changing the setting back and forth will often correct this problem.

If all these measures fail to produce the expected results, take the meter to the repair shop, or look into companies specializing in meter repair that offer both quick turnaround times and often low prices. Another option if you have a broken built-in meter is to buy a handheld meter with the money you would otherwise be spending on the repair.

Faulty aperture setting or mechanism. Sometimes, what we set is not what we get. In most SLRs, the lens stays open at its maximum aperture until the shutter releases and automatically stops down to the designated aperture setting during the exposure, then opens up to maximum aperture for viewing. With the lens on the camera, set the aperture to the one you used in your film test, and wind and release the shutter several times. If the lens is not stopping down at all, remove the lens and inspect the aperture linkage (see your camera's instruction manual) to see if it is damaged or not moving freely. On some electronic cameras there are electrical contacts operating the meter and aperture that need to be clean to work properly. Others have locking mechanisms that disable the aperture for specialized purposes. Make sure that everything is set properly, reinstall the lens, and repeat the test.

There should be no play in the lens mount at all. If there is, check the tightness of the screws on both the camera mount and the back of the lens. Remount the lens and check for any play (which could disable the aperture mechanism or produce erratic movement of the aperture leaves). If the mount seems solid but the aperture varies in size for any fixed setting, or is sluggish in its action or sticks in any position, then you have a $60 problem to solve before the lens is useful again.

All the above. This is just a reminder that your camera and meter may be suffering from more than one problem. This series of checks takes only a minute or two to perform, so it is best to do them all. It is also a good idea to do these tests with your camera on a regular basis, and especially before starting your shooting session.

Checking Sharpness
Are Your Slides the Cutting Edge?

It is hard to judge critical sharpness of 35mm transparencies with the unaided eye. At $1 \times 1^1/_2$ inches, they are just too small. Placing a lupe (a magnifying glass) directly on top of the slide mount will enable you to see an enlarged image. The larger the image, the easier it is to determine its apparent sharpness. The fixed magnification of most lupes will range from four times to ten times life-size (indicated as 4X, 5X, and so on).

Quite popular is an inexpensive plastic 8X lupe, which enlarges the image the same ratio as an 8×12-inch print. You won't be able to see the whole image at one time with this 8X lupe, so you must move it around on the slide mount to check the sharpness edge to edge. Just remember that this is a *plastic* optic with all of the associated shortcomings (color aberrations, dispersion, and astigmatism). A high-quality lupe with well-corrected glass optics will cost nearly as much as a lens for your camera, but it will produce the best image quality.

Or you can just use the normal lens off your camera as your

lupe (magnification will vary with focal length). Remove the lens from the camera body and hold it, with the front facing you, just above the transparency on the light box. Adjusting the height that you are holding the lens will vary the magnification slightly. You can easily improvise a collar to attach to the back of the lens that will hold it at the correct height. Either way, be sure that you don't touch the transparency itself because the surface is fragile.

Sharpness Troubleshooting

There are only a few major causes of loss of sharpness. Check each item in order.

Stabilize the camera. The most likely cause of poor sharpness is that the camera was not held steadily enough by you or your tripod during the exposure. Make sure all tripod adjustments are tightly locked, use your self-timer or a good cable release, lock the mirror up if possible, and eliminate all environmental vibration. If problems persist, use higher shutter speeds and try hanging some extra weight from the center column of your tripod. The weight creates more inertia and a steadier platform for your camera.

Focus critically. Sometimes it's pretty easy to simply miss the focus, especially in dim light. Many professionals use a separate, high-powered raw light on the object just while they are focusing. Many cameras have attachments that flip into place over the eyepiece that will magnify the image (like a lupe) when you look into the viewfinder. If you need glasses to see things at distance, you must wear them while focusing or use a correction eyepiece on your camera.

Select the correct aperture. Choosing the right aperture is very critical with three-dimensional work. It is necessary to use a small enough aperture to ensure adequate sharpness over the entire object. Use the depth-of-field indicator on the lens (see page 17). Focus the lens about one-third the distance behind the front of the object. Use as small an aperture as possible. With flat artwork, focus becomes less critical as the aperture gets smaller.

Check the viewfinder. If you have already checked everything above, the problem may be in your camera. Alignment of the lens, mirror, and pentaprism is very critical. It doesn't take much to push the alignment out. Have it looked at by a reliable repair shop.

Color Balance
An Opposing Solution

It is impossible to judge color balance accurately unless you have the correct exposure and proper density in your transparency. Unless there is a gross color error in your test shot that will clearly point you in one very obvious direction, don't try to adjust the color until you get the correct exposure in one of your brackets.

Most E-6 transparency films, which the vast majority of readers of this book will be using exclusively, pick up a cool tone (green or blue) if underexposed, and often exhibit this coolness in the shadow areas, too. These casts disappear in transparencies that are properly exposed. And all transparency films exhibit murky and unrealistic colors overall whenever underexposed by one or more stops. The film's colors are designed to be accurate and balanced only when properly exposed. You cannot begin to make any assessment of the color quality if all your film is underexposed.

Overexposure creates its own problems in judging color balance since it lightens everything (decreases the overall density), eliminating color shifts that would otherwise be apparent if it were properly exposed. If you can't see it, how can you correct it?

There are only two ways to change color in your film: *Filtration* and *exposure*.

To understand the principle of filtration, put on a pair of green sunglasses, and carefully notice how the world takes on a greenish tinge. Although the change may be quite subtle, the effect is the addition of a distinct cast that is uniform throughout the field of view. We can do the same thing by attaching a similarly colored filter to the front of the camera lens.

To understand exposure, compare the color of a clear blue sky with and without a dark pair of neutral gray sunglasses. Without the glasses, the sky is light blue; with the glasses, it appears dark blue. The only difference is the amount of light transmitted to your eye. The same thing happens on film. In fact, you can change any solid color photographed simply by underexposing or overexposing your film.

Filters and Filtration
Seeing the Art World Behind Magenta-Colored Glasses

Most amateurs rarely, if ever, use or own filters. If you don't already own one, it is a good idea to buy either a skylight or UV (ultraviolet) haze filter. Both are essentially clear and are designed to stop all ultraviolet light from passing through the filter. This is a good thing, since film is sensitive to UV light and will record this generally as increased atmospheric haze that is invisible to humans. It also serves as lens protection from the weather and scratching, and is a lot cheaper to replace if damaged than replacing the lens.

Professionals use filtration to make small but significant corrections to the overall color in their photographs. They usually use filters that are designated by density (how much light they block as opposed to how much they transmit) and color. The density is expressed as a percentage, and the color is abbreviated to its first letter. Therefore, a filter marked 10Y is yellow with a density of 10 percent, a filter marked 40B is blue with a density of 40 percent, and so on. The larger the number, the greater the color shift. The smallest density on the market is 2.5 percent, which subtly alters color balance on film. In actuality, the 5, 10, and 20 percent filters are about the only ones you need, and these can be combined to produce heavier densities (all three would produce a color density of 35 percent, but expect 5 to 10 percent higher than that in overall density due to stacking inefficiencies).

Combining more than three filters isn't a good idea because optical quality will suffer. Be sure to obtain an exposure-compensating chart from the filter manufacturer. Using a 40M filter requires about one full f-stop extra exposure.

Filter Types
Some Filters Are More Equal Than Others

There are two types of color-compensating filters (or CC filters) that you can use on your lens. One is a screw-in filter that fits the threads on the end of your lens; these are generally the most expensive. Buying a complete set will reduce the per-filter cost somewhat, but be prepared to spend several hundred dollars for this option.

The other type is a gel CC filter that is 3 or 4 inches square. These are quite fragile and are attached to the camera via a gel holder. Most professional photographers go this route because they can attach the gel holder, via adapters, to a wide range of cameras and lenses (this saves the photographer from having a dozen different sets of filters).

Some camera manufacturers don't standardize the filter thread size for their typical everyday lenses. In this instance, buy the filter or gel holder for the largest diameter lens you plan to use and buy reducing, or step-down, rings to attach them to lenses that have smaller filter diameters (if you attached a smaller filter to a lens of wider diameter the filter ring may intrude in the frame area producing darkened corners, an effect called vignetting). I suggest that you buy your gels as you need them, unless they are hard to come by in your area.

If you are in a situation where you don't have the correct CC gel, you can substitute color printing gels as a makeshift replacement. These gels are made to provide filtration of the light source in color enlargers while making color prints. In this situation, the gels are not normally placed in the image path (in this case between the enlarger lens and the printing paper) so that it doesn't need to meet the same optical standard as CC gels (placed between object and lens). They are much cheaper, however, and come in a set so complete that it will cover almost every imaginable photographic situation; and you may be hard pressed to tell the difference.

Kodak Wratten Filters

At most amateur camera stores, the only color correction filters available are screw mounts made of optical glass, or lately optical plastic, with Kodak Wratten filter designations. Warming filters all have the number 81 followed by A, B, C, and so on. The 82 Wratten series all have a bluish cast that changes in 100°K increments with each successive letter designation, starting with A. A "straight" 82 filter shifts the color temperature exactly 100°K cooler, while the 82A shifts exactly 200°K cooler. An 82C shifts the color temperature 400°K cooler. These numbers are added to the measured color temperature. For example, if the light is measured to be 2800°K, an 82C would add 400°K to make a total of 3200°K, the correct color balance for most tungsten films. These filters can also be used with daylight film to eliminate the general reddishness of photos taken very late or very early in the day (the first hour after sunrise, the last hour before sunset).

Warming filters all have the number 81 followed by A, B, C, and so on. As the letters progresses alphabetically, subtract 100°K from the color temperature. These filters are useful for eliminating bluish casts caused by small electronic flash units, snow scenes, heavy overcast, etc. It is also eliminates the bluish cast in shadow areas when using high speed E-6 films. and high-speed color.

Use the following chart to correct color with filters:

TOO BLUE	ADD YELLOW
TOO GREEN	ADD MAGENTA
TOO RED	ADD CYAN

OR VICE VERSA

TOO YELLOW	ADD BLUE
TOO MAGENTA	ADD GREEN
TOO CYAN	ADD RED

Using the color correction chart above, by trial and error, you will come up with the right filter to use. A color viewing guide makes this task simple and virtually foolproof. The Kodak guide I use has six (there are others available with up to twenty-four) closely spaced cut-outs on a 5 × 7-inch card with red, magenta, yellow, cyan, green, and blue gels, each at 10 percent density. It easy and quick to look through one gel after another and choose the one that makes the image look perfect. You will need to add the same amount and color of filtration during the next shoot to get the same result on film.

Sometimes, you may not see anything that looks perfect through the viewing guide, but there will be one filter that makes it look better. You now know the proper color to add and only have to work out the proper increase in density.

Common Problems in Choosing the Right Filtration
Eyes, Don't Fail Me Now

Knowing how to achieve the right filtration may be difficult in the beginning and may take some experience to master. The receptors in your eyes are fast in adapting to any illumination, so that any offending cast seems to disappear if you look at it too long. Quick scans to and from the transparency work the best, but be careful not to look at a bright area in between (another good reason for blocking out unused areas on your light box). This keeps your eye from adjusting to any one source of light and makes it easier to note any differences.

You will be amazed at how your color perception improves the more you practice. You may even see the world different-ly—noticing that snow on a clear day is not only white but has the blue sky reflected in it or that players on a golf green pick up a greenish cast.

It may be worth the time and expense to do a special film test if you continue to have trouble judging color balance. Take a picture of a large photo-gray card and a color scale that has large blocks of standardized, accurately reproduced color. These are cheap and readily available at any good camera store. If you are doing flat work, place the color scale where you would normally place your art and follow the same shooting protocol. If you are shooting three-dimensional art, place the color scale so that it is evenly illuminated with no glare. I do this every time I test a new batch of film (using the two-light method, figure 3.2) to see how good it is or what I need to do to make it better. The neutral gray card (18 percent reflectance) and the white band in the color chart will point out any unwanted cast. Take as many test shots as needed, until the exposure and filtration make all the colors and gray card repro-duce accurately on film. The artwork you shoot in the same light will usually turn out spot on.

The Second Test
If at First You Don't Succeed . . .

If everything went right on your first test and the color is cor-rected, there is no need for a second test. If you made only one copy of each in your test and want additional copies, review your notes and use the exposure setting that produced the best result (no need to bracket). If you have the time, you can perform a test on your lab by sending them one more roll for processing and then compare the results.

If you see any discrepancy in color or density, point it out to the lab and show them your clearly marked results. There will always be some slight fluctuations in any processing system, but these should stay within fairly narrow parameters. Any decent lab processes control strips of film (carefully exposed and handled by the manufacturer) that allow them to track and precisely measure the results and correct film speed and color. Ask them to show you the test for the day or time that the film was processed and explain the differences. Large differences in color or density are inexcusable and you may want to investigate another lab.

If you have to make just a slight color correction (either 5 percent or 10 percent density), you can probably go ahead and finish your shoot as described above (with the same caveat regarding processing). If you need more than a 10 percent correction, it is much safer to do a second test, since often what you see by looking through heavier filters is not what you actually get on film.

If you don't want to use another whole roll for this test, make your exposure bracket (be sure to compensate for any filter factor) and shoot about six frames. Put the lens cap on and shoot two more frames. This moves your last image 3 inches inside your camera and onto the take-up spool. Now you can go into a completely dark room (such as a closet, with a towel blocking the space between the floor and the door, that is next to a dim adjoining room) to remove the film. Put a pair of scissors in one pocket, an empty film canister in another. Sitting with the camera in your lap, push the rewind button and turn out the light.

You can now open the camera back and pull the film cassette out slightly to facilitate cutting the film close to the cassette. Let the camera rest on your lap and pull the advanced film off the take-up spool, wrapping it tightly enough to fit into the film canister. Do not turn on the light until you are certain the canister cap is on tight. Tape the top so that you (or anyone else) won't open it up accidentally. Put it in an envelope and label it as loose film.

Be sure to also mark the envelope with any processing instructions and the type of film enclosed (since the lab won't be able to refer to the cassette for this information). All you need to do to use the rest of the film cartridge is pull out just enough film to cut a similar tongue (look at another unused roll if you can't figure it out) and put it back into your camera. You will have about twenty-four shots left on a thirty-six-exposure roll.

This whole process is simple and I have used it for years whenever I had to test a new emulsion. I use a grease pencil to mark the frames left on the cartridge and put it into another film canister, again marking the lid with the number of exposures left. I save this partial roll to use for another film test or for a job that requires a smaller number of frames (thirty-six-exposures per roll is always cheaper per frame than twenty-four exposures per roll). Just remember film is very sensitive and it only takes a little light to fog and ruin loose film—so handle it only in the dark.

Evaluating Second Test Shots
Meanwhile Back at the Light Box . . .

Label your second test shots with the date, f-stop, and filtration, and arrange them on the light box next to your original test shots for comparison. If the second shots look good, you can finish your shoot. If you have overcorrected, compare your first test with the second and visualize what the halfway point between the two would look like. If you made a 10 percent shift for your second test, the halfway point is 5 percent and it is pretty safe to finish your shoot and be assured of your results. If you made a 30 percent change for your second test, the halfway point is 15 percent. It's a good idea to run another test for optimal results.

If you have undercorrected on your second test, use your first test to project what doubling your filtration would look like. If you think the new correction will work, do another test, making sure to compensate for exposure loss due to filter density. You may want to try a few different filter packs to speed up the process. Let's say you used 10 percent filtration in your second test. You can shoot a test with 20 percent filtration, as well as 15 and 25 percent filtrations, using the same f-stop and shutter speed. Pick the perfect photographic result and you are ready.

Persistent Problems
You Cut It Twice and It's Still Too Short

If your corrections don't seem to be helping at all, go back to the basics because most often it's the little things that trip us up, such as not waiting twenty more minutes until nightfall so that it was absolutely dark before reshooting; or forgetting to roll up the lime-green area rug next to your lights, thereby filling the frame with the same lovely color; or leaving the exposed film on a hot radiator overnight. Having to do reshoots is frustrating, so keep your attention focused.

Review of the System for Ultimate Color Correction

The following, in outline form, is everything you need to do to achieve total control when photographing in your studio. Use it as a checklist while setting up or while troubleshooting.

Master Plan for Color-Correct Slides

1. Good Film Stock

from reliable source

correctly stored

pretested (known color balance)

properly exposed

promptly processed

2. Camera and Lens

appropriate film properly loaded

accurate (or tested) shutter speeds

flash: synch test

individual color characteristic of lens
(any change of lens may produce a color shift)

reciprocity effects speed and color

proper filtration attached

3. Lighting Equipment

tested for each film stock

corrected for bulb aging

assumes: same bulb, same reflector, same umbrella
(or any other diffusion material)

4. Environmental Factors

backdrop color tested

ambient and conflicting light eliminated

age and color of reflecting material correct

correction or testing of overall environment

5. Processing

send in test roll or clip test for color and speed

check lab testing procedures

run rest of film in the very next run

color shifts for pulling (cooler) and for pushing (warmer)

6. Viewing

on color-correct light box

with matte cut out to block out extra light

projection: typical viewing setup

handholding: best and worst scenario
of viewing slide pages

Projecting Your Slides

If you have done a good job and produced the perfect transparency, you can reward yourself with the ultimate photographic treat, and project your art onto a screen in a darkened room.

Just keep in mind that slides always look better projected, making it harder to judge them critically. Here again, the human eye adapts readily to the prevailing illumination, automatically masking all the minor color corrections needed. A typical projector's lens masks a whole host of other transparency deficiencies by producing image flare and thereby lowering overall sharpness and contrast.

Proper density is also difficult to accurately judge by projection, since different projector models have different light-quantity outputs. The brightness of the image is also determined by the distance projected (an image projected twice as far by the same projector is four times dimmer) and the reflectance of the screen or surface. Projection bulbs have a long life, but in their "twilight" years they get progressively dimmer, adding yet another variable.

Choosing the Right Projection Transparency
Don't Throw Any of Them Away—Yet

In general, normal to slightly darker than normal slides usually project the best and are least likely to have burned-out highlights—the plague of all bad transparencies. But again, that will depend on your projection setup. One client has me divide and mark her exposure bracket of transparencies into two categories: appropriate for projection and reproduction, and appropriate for viewing in frosted slide pages.

Unfortunately, most of your art slides will be viewed under whatever illumination is handy at the moment by someone holding a slide page up to a light. Make sure to put them in pages with frosted backing (this both diffuses the light and throws whatever is in the background way out of focus). Normal and slightly lighter slides generally look better in slide pages under most lighting conditions. Test this out for yourself under a variety of situations and choose accordingly.

I like to show my slides in something a bit fancier than a slide sheet. A number of manufacturers produce 8 × 10-inch and 11 × 14-inch boards that hold twelve mounted transparencies. The slides are mounted to the back of the board, so that what you see from the front is the image area alone. The board is slipped into a sleeve that has a frosted back. The overall presentation is neat and professional, and, along with being easier to view, commands a bit more respect.

You will be miles ahead if you can get the persons you want to see your work to view projected slides. Plan ahead. If they don't have a projector, bring your own, as well as a screen. Make sure they have a darkened room or arrive as it is getting dark. Choose the optimum slide exposure for the projector and test it out. Make the most of their undivided attention in the most optimum conditions you can provide.

Acknowledgments

Since this is the first book I have written, I have a lot of people to thank. Here they are, in no particular order:

My mother and father for having me; my dogs for their spiritual guidance; my sisters for not killing me as I grew up; Lars Perrson for not letting me kill myself while learning how to fly; Walt Craig and all my other photo teachers for their patience and encouragement; Ish Peres and Harolto Alves for their impatience with anything less than perfection; Betty Woodman for getting me started in this business; Garth Clark for keeping me going; Anne Edelstein for getting this book published; Crown for publishing this book; and all the artists that made the art I had the pleasure to photograph.

I would like to thank Rob Abernathy, Gretchen Atkins, Mark Del Vecchio, David McFadden, Sandy Brant, Bob Ellison, Gene Hecht, Marty Shack, Yvonne Muranushi, Leah Holmes Ramirez, Sharon Gallagher, Constance Hearndon, Buffy Easton, Bill Ehrlich, Julie Rauer, Walter and Caren Forbes, Maria Friedrich, Nick Cerrulli, Ron Schreier, Deborah O'Brien, and Joe Fornabaio for being a pleasure to work with.

Four gold stars and my eternal indebtedness go to Sharon Squibb for her patience, and for putting up with me in general. In particular, I wish to thank her for making this a much better book with her careful and meticulous editing. I would also like to thank Jessica Arendt for helping me get this book started, and her pre-edit of the first five chapters.

And a final thanks to the memory of Walter Schladen, my composition teacher in college who taught me how to express myself in all areas of my life. I'm sorry that I never got to thank him again in person.

Illustration Credits

Front cover: Painting by Kathleen Gilje; Ceramic by Peter Gourfain; page 33, Sharon Seifert; page 127, Jill Schwartz/Elements.

Index

Entries in <u>italics</u> refer to figures and illustrations.